INTERVIEWS WITH

Oscar Ichazo

ARICA INSTITUTE PRESS · NEW YORK

ACKNOWLEDGMENTS

"We have no desire to strengthen the ego or make it happy" by Sam Keen, Copyright 1973, is reprinted with permission from *Psychology Today* magazine, Ziff-Davis Publishing Company. "Pears interviews Oscar" Parts I and II by Antonio Huneeus, is reprinted with permission from *Pears of Aphrodite* magazine, Washington, D.C. "A talk with Oscar Ichazo" by Rick Fields, Copyright 1976, is reprinted with permission from *New Age* magazine, by New Age Communications, Inc. "Making a Mystical School" and "The Mission of Arica" by Susan Lydon, are reprinted with permission from the *No Time Times* newspaper, New York. "Interview with Oscar Ichazo" by Karimu Kudura, and "A fireside chat" by Oscar Ichazo, are reprinted with permission from the *Inside* journal, P.O. Box 3162, Eugene, Oregon 97403. "I am the root of a new tradition" by Dorothy De Christopher, Copyright 1981, is reprinted with permission from *The Movement Newspaper*, MSIA, P.O. Box 19458, Los Angeles, California 90019.

First Edition

Published by Arica Institute Press
235 Park Avenue South, New York, New York 10003

Library of Congress Catalogue Card Number: 81-70539

ISBN 0-916554-02-3 (hard cover)
ISBN 0-916554-03-1 (paper cover)

Printed in the United States of America by
Fairfield Graphics, Fairfield, Pennsylvania
Set in ITC Garamond
Design by Frank Mangis and Prisha D'Andrade

INTERVIEWS WITH
Oscar Ichazo

CONTENTS

FOREWORD

EVEN BEFORE the fifty-seven Americans went to Chile to begin work with Oscar Ichazo, he had begun to use the interview format to supply information. After the first flurry of letters back and forth, Oscar asked us to get together as a group and supply him with a list of questions. Though he answered each question directly, even more important than the direct answers were the cadenzas or variations on the themes of the questions, which revealed to us the limited dimensions of our thinking.

He does much the same in these interviews. Once the interviewer has established his general terrain of interest, Oscar occupies it with tranquil authority.

His view of the terrain, however, is multileveled, and in describing it, he stretches our conventional understanding. Oscar speaks with disarming directness and simplicity about such concepts as metaphysics and the transcendental, about science and mysticism as seen in the light of this moment of history.

JOHN BLEIBTREU

Arlington, Vermont
November, 1981

BREAKING THE TYRANNY OF THE EGO

Interview by Sam Keen, 1973

WHEN THE DEATH of God was announced a few years back some believers and some skeptics suspected He might pop back to life before long. Gods survive better than atheists; they disappear in the winter of our disillusionment, change shapes and costumes, and are resurrected in the spring. If the prophets and gurus of the consciousness revolution are to be believed, God has been reborn and we are rapidly approaching the Omega Point, the Great Awakening, the New Age of the Spirit.

Even to the skeptical observer, a new religious sensitivity is obvious in the widespread interest in Transcendental Meditation, yoga, Sufism, Scientology and the occult arts. Scores of roshis, lamas, swamis, fourteen-year-old perfect masters, middle-aged wise men and other realized beings are criss-crossing the United States dispensing a new religion to eager audiences. All this may be a fad. Or we may be at the beginning of a religious reformation more radical than anything that has happened in the West since Calvin got married to Capitalism and gave birth to the modern industrial state.

Despite considerable differences, the advocates of the new religion agree in their rejection of the limited view of consciousness that has characterized Western culture. The human

---

Sam Keen. "We have no desire to strengthen the ego or make it happy." An interview with Oscar Ichazo. *Psychology Today*. July, 1973.

mind is not a machine enclosed within a series of constricting Chinese boxes—the head, the body, the environment, the historical moment. It is nothing less than a part of the Divine Intelligence that is homogenized into the entire cosmos. Man, the argument goes, is a cosmological rather than a psychological animal. We are spirit within Spirit, consciousness within Consciousness, void within Void, atman within Brahman, god within God. With the resurgence of a cosmic definition of consciousness comes a rejection of the dualisms that have haunted the Judeo-Christian world: God and man, the supernatural and the natural, the sacred and the secular, faith and reason, science (psychology) and religion.

The new religion is challenging the psychological approach to understanding and curing human dis-ease. It is offering both a new anthropology and a new therapeutic, which begin with the assumption that psychology is a manifestation of the disease for which it purports to be the cure.

As a separate science, psychology was born as God was dying in the nineteenth century. Once Christianity had chased the great god Pan from the wild places of nature and the machine drove him from the heavens, man's only hope of saving himself came from within his psyche. The ego was assigned the role of the missing God. And this, according to the new gurus, is the problem. If we begin with the premise that man is an alien in the cosmos, then all we can do is strengthen the walls that keep us within our self-imposed prisons and learn to cope with loneliness. But true therapy consists in ridding ourselves of the illusion of individuality and dissolving our egocentrism in cosmic consciousness.

There is no better place to savor the distilled essence of the new religious consciousness than the Arica Institute. Arica opened its doors in New York in 1971 to seventy-six people; most of whom had heard of the teachings of its founder, Oscar Ichazo, from a group of Esalen pilgrims who had been at the original school in Arica, Chile. In two years Arica has grown to have a staff of 250 teachers, centers in New York, San Francisco, and Los Angeles, and training programs in a dozen other cities. The curriculum of the School is an amalgam of techniques and disciplines taken from esoteric and religious traditions of the East and West that have been streamlined to give modern Americans a practical path toward almost guaranteed enlightenment. At the New York headquarters an escalator whisks students and visitors up through a draped tunnel to a carpeted suite of rooms that are colorfully decorated with symbols—Tarot cards, yin-yang, diagrams of the levels of satori. Here meditation, mantras, mudras, eurythmics, drumming, yoga, and the latest encounter and group techniques are mixed with lectures on philosophy and diet to form a system of thought and practice that raises the consciousness of the group to a state of enlightenment.

Oscar Ichazo talks with assurance about the coming revolution in consciousness and about the hope that Arica can train sufficient teachers to help the new awakening happen fast enough to save Western culture from the death toward which it is otherwise speeding. The facts he chooses to reveal about his life and training are few and misty. His expert knowledge of the maps of human consciousness and ancient and modern techniques for traveling in psychic space is obvious. Although Arica is largely the result of his vision, he is gradually receding into the background as the organization and spiritual technology he has created begin the job of teaching the mysteries of the higher consciousness which is aborning.

SAM KEEN: In the Arica Institute you seem to have created the nearest thing we now have to a university for altered states of consciousness. In your curriculum I can spot ego-reducing and consciousness-raising techniques borrowed from Zen, Sufism, Buddhism, psychoanalysis, encounter, the Gurdjieff work, and many others. How did you come to be a master and teacher of such a large variety of different techniques from so many different religious and esoteric traditions?

OSCAR ICHAZO: That's a long story. Arica is not as much my invention as it is a product of our times. The knowledge I have contributed to the School came to me from many sources I encountered in my peculiar quest. You might say that I began my exploration of consciousness not to reach altered states of awareness but to escape from them. But that story begins very early in childhood.

Q: Then, let's begin there.

OSCAR: I was raised in Bolivia and Peru. My parents were formally Roman Catholic but had no deep religious interest. I went to a Jesuit school and learned about the theology of the church. Then, quite suddenly, I began to have attacks which came at those moments when I was between waking and sleeping. The first time it happened (on December 20, 1937) I was six and a half years old. The attacks were very violent, not epileptic, but like that. First, I would experience a lot of pain and the fear that I was going to die, and my heart would pound. Then it would stop, the pain would increase and I would die. After a while I would return to my body and discover that I was alive. These attacks began to happen every two or three days. I was terrified but I knew my parents couldn't help me so I didn't say anything to them. I became very lonely and felt different from everyone else. I was constantly afraid that the next attack would be the last, or that my parents might think I was dead when I was only out of my body, so I worried obsessively about how I might return to normality.

Q: Were the images and visions you saw when you were out of your body pleasurable or painful?

OSCAR: Both. When you are in your astral body, both fear and ecstasy can be multiplied to infinite proportions because there are no limits within pure consciousness. It was this that led to my first disillusionment with the church. When the priest taught about Hell, I would say to myself, "Last night I was in Hell and it wasn't like that." And the paradise of the church didn't come any closer to the one I saw in my travels. Still, I thought Communion and prayer might help me get rid of my fearful obsession, but they only made it worse. I was like a man who took LSD with the hope that something miraculous would happen and...nothing. Prayer only made me focus more firmly on my problem.

Q: How did you begin to circle out of your obsession?

OSCAR: I made the discovery that being caught in my own subjectivity was hell and there were things I could do to get me out of hell.

Q: After the standard means of grace failed, you took responsibility for the control of your own consciousness.

OSCAR: A little bit. At least the idea was there, but it took me many years to gain the control. I started reading everything I could find on anatomy, physiology, and medicine with the hope of finding out what to do about my condition. Then I had the good fortune to be introduced to the martial arts. I started samurai training and had my first introduction to Zen meditation. My family owned some land, so I had contact with the Indians and they introduced me to psychedelic drugs and shamanism while I was in my early teens. I also began to experiment with hypnotism and to practice yoga. And all the while I was reading all the philosophy I could get ahold of—especially William James. At seventeen, I went to the University at La Paz, but I was bored and disappointed and very much alone.

Q: The tension is building, so we must be getting near the punch line.

OSCAR: When I was nineteen, a remarkable man found me in La Paz. He was sixty years old and when he began to teach me, I knew from the beginning that he was speaking the truth. This man, whose name I have pledged not to reveal, belonged to a small group in Buenos Aires that met to share their knowledge of various esoteric consciousness-altering techniques. I became the coffee boy for this group. I would get up at four A.M. to make their coffee and breakfast and would stay around as inconspicuously as possible. Gradually they got used to my presence and they started using me as a guinea pig to demonstrate techniques to each other. To settle arguments about whether some particular kind of meditation or mantra worked, they would have me try it and report what I experienced.

Q: What kinds of disciplines were being shared in the group?

OSCAR: About two-thirds of the group were Orientals, so they were strong on Zen, Sufism, and Kaballah. They also used some techniques I later found in the Gurdjieff work.

Q: Where does the story go from here?

OSCAR: One day when I was serving coffee, an argument arose between two members of the group. I turned to one and said, "You are not right. He is right." Just like that. Then I explained the point until both of them understood. This incident changed everything. They asked me to leave, and I thought I was being kicked out for being pretentious. But after about a week, they called me back and told me they had all decided to teach me. They worked with me for two more years and then opened doors for me in the Orient. After a time of remaining at home in Chile, I began to travel and study in the East, in Hong Kong, India, and Tibet. I did more work in the martial arts, learned all of the higher yogas, studied Buddhism, and Confucianism, alchemy, and the wisdom of the *I Ching.* Then I went back to La Paz to live with my father and digest my learnings. After working alone for a year, I went into a divine coma for seven days. When I came out of it I knew that I should teach; it was impossible that all my good luck should be only for myself. But it took me two years to act on this decision. Then I went to Santiago and started lecturing in the Institute for Applied Psychology. Things got so busy and crowded there that I decided to move to the remote little town of Arica and filter out all except the really committed persons who would follow me there. At first I worked with a group of ten. Then in 1970, a group of Americans—about fifty—came and stayed for nine months. Fifteen of these were from Esalen. It was clear to me that the time had come to move the work to North America. So here we are—the Arica Institute with centers in New York, Los Angeles, and San Francisco.

Q: Every form of therapy, whether it is carried on in churches, growth centers, consulting rooms or wisdom schools rests upon a vision of what man might become, a diagnosis of his present unhappiness and a prescription for how he may move toward fulfillment. What kind of an animal is a human being?

OSCAR: We have to distinguish between man as he is in essence, and as he is in ego or personality. In essence, every person is perfect, fearless, and in a loving unity with the entire cosmos; there is no conflict within the person between head, heart, and stomach or between the person and others. Every human being starts in pure essence. Then something happens: the ego begins to develop; karma accumulates; there is a transition from objectivity to subjectivity; man falls from essence into personality.

Q: Is the fall a historical incident? Or are you talking about some mythical event like the expulsion from the Garden of Eden, or the class conflict that developed when the bourgeois began to exploit the proletariat, or the childhood replay of the drama of Oedipus or Electra?

OSCAR: A person retains the purity of essence for a short time. It is lost between four and six years of age when the child begins to imitate his parents, tell lies, and pretend. A contradiction develops between the inner feelings of the child and the outer social reality to which he must conform. Ego consciousness is the limited mode of awareness that develops as a result of the fall into society. Personality forms a defensive layer over the essence, and so there is a split between the self and the world. The ego feels the world as alien and dangerous because it constantly fails to satisfy the deeper needs of the self.

Q: Erik Erikson describes the same process as the failure to maintain a relationship of basic trust. Society is based upon that mild form of schizophrenia we call 'normality'.

OSCAR: Another way to characterize the ego is as the principle of compensation for an imagined loss. When we turn away from our primal perfection, our completeness, our unity with the world and God, we create the illusion that we need something exterior to ourselves for our completion. This dependency on what is exterior is what makes man's ego. Once man is within ego consciousness he is driven by desire and fear. He can find no real happiness until desire is extinguished and he returns to his essence, that is, until he reaches what Buddhism called nirvana or the void.

Q: The question of desire seems to be the crucial point that separates Eastern and Western visions of man. Buddhism and Eastern religion in general see desire as something that must be purged before man can be happy, but Western philosophers and psychologists tend to believe that if we can separate our conscious and unconscious desires we can strengthen the ego to deal with reality and achieve happiness. I think Plato's myth of the birth of erotic love is archetypical for the Western mind. Originally human beings were joined back to back in pairs. Pairs came in three varieties, male-male, female-female, male-female. The gods took compassion on them and split them apart so they could face each other and make love. Erotic love is the drive to be reunited with our lost half. We desire because we are incomplete. The deepest root of desire is the natural dependency between the sexes. Isn't desire rooted in biological differences, in the ontological fact of the incompleteness? Why not accept the need for interdependence, rather than try to purge the ego and root out desire for what delights and completes us? Aren't you trying to make the self independent of the world?

OSCAR: No. Only of a certain artificially constructed social world. The illusory world that Buddhism spoke of as maya—illusion—is a socially created idea of what the world is. It is one way of seeing things. So long as we remain within the ego, we see the world only through the screen of our fears, our vanity, and our desire.

Q: And if we shatter the illusions of the ego, we can, as Don Juan said, "stop the world" and discover reality. If the ego is the devil in man it would be good to understand what it is made up of and how it works. What is this ego you are trying to remove from modern man?

OSCAR: Since ego is false or distorted consciousness, the best way to define it is to back up a step and look more closely at man's essential nature. There are three centers in the human animal: the intellectual, the emotional, and the vital—or as we call them: the path, the oth, and the kath. Ideally the kath is the master of life; it is the center which directs vital movement and allows us to relate to the world with instinctual immediacy. We sense our basic unity with all life in our guts.

This idea is common to many wisdom traditions. In the Orient, the martial arts concentrated on developing awareness of this center, which they located about four inches below the navel. They called it the *tan t'ien* or the *hara*.

Q: And the oth center would be the one traditionally connected with the heart?

OSCAR: Yes. And reason with the path. In short, what happens when ego develops is that the head takes over and tries to direct everything. The ego is made up of words and ideas, endless interior chatter, and repetitious thought patterns that form fixed ways of defending the person against the natural flow of life. Ego creates a whole subjective world that must be defended against objective reality, so it always exists in fear.

Q: The fundamental human problem, then, is the existence of ego. What is the prescription that will lead us back to health and essence?

OSCAR: Ego is made up of three interconnected parts: it has an intellectual segment, an emotional segment, and a movement segment. Ego reduction involves working with each of these elements. The way we do this in Arica is rather intricate. Do you want the whole theory and practice of ego reduction?

Q: Well, the best Freud could promise was interminable analysis to strengthen the ego so we could cope with the everlasting discontent of the real world, and most other Western therapeutics promise only improvement or adjustment. So, if you are suggesting that we might be cured of ego altogether, I am interested in hearing the details.

OSCAR: Let's begin with the intellectual aspect of the ego.

The difficulty is both that we are always trying to control life with our heads and that so long as we remain in ego we have the wrong ideas about man and his place in the cosmos. Very early in our training we introduce a system of mentations that trains people to think with their entire bodies rather than only with their 'minds'.

It is a mistake to consider thought the result of one specialized organ, the brain. If there are no internal blocks set up by the ego, each thought is as much a product of the eye or the foot as of the brain-computer. When we are unified, thought and action are the same. We divide the body into twelve parts, each of which has a physiological and a parallel psychological function:

Ears perceive the meaning or logos and give us
the substance of things.
Eyes isolate forms.
The nose smells out possibilities.
The mouth and the stomach sense our needs
for nourishment.
The heart energizes the organism with its impulse.
The liver assimilates food and percepts we take into
the organism.
The colon, anus, bladder, and kidneys eliminate foods,
ideas, and experiences that are unmetabolizable.
The genitals reflect our orientation toward or away from life.
The thighs and upper arms reflect our capacity, or strength.
The knees and elbows reflect the ease or awkwardness,
the charisma, with which we move through the world.
The calves and forearms are the means we use.
The hands and feet are used for going and taking,
for reaching out for goals.

Q: How does this technique work? If, for instance, I were considering whether I should get a serious job or take off for Tahiti, would I begin with my goals and think the problem through with all of the other parts of my body?

OSCAR: That is one way the mentations are used. Any question or problem you are considering can be thought through more completely by allowing each part of the body to become infused with consciousness. There are also times when you become specially aware of some part of the body. If, for instance, you are having trouble with your kidneys, you need to ask what things in your life must be eliminated. More generally, the mentations are used to condition the entire body to tune itself to the world. Once consciousness is homogenized into the entire organism, the head is emptied and it ceases to exert a tyrannical control over everything.

Q: The idea of overthrowing the domination of the head and spreading consciousness more democratically in other parts of the body—participatory democracy in the body and the body politic—seems to be emerging in many different places these days. Norman O. Brown wants to see us have "polymorphously perverse" bodies, Don Juan's "man of knowledge" has fibers of light that connect his solar plexus to the world, and the advocates of Zen are inviting us to practice "no mind." A lot of people in Western culture are tired of mind-tripping, and look to the body as the new Eden. But if we have to lose our heads to find our tails we are only flipping the coin. I sometimes think we are in danger of forgetting what Plato and Aristotle taught us—the mind is an erogenous zone. We need to use it more to caress and care for the world and less to manipulate it.

OSCAR: I would agree. We are not anti-intellectual. The techniques we use are designed only to destroy ego-dominated thought. We believe there are ideas a person must understand in order to be whole. Not only must we change the way we think but we must change what we think. We call the intellectual part of the ego the fixation, and each fixation is remedied by an idea. Every person develops a style of compensating for the lack, the ontological emptiness, which is at the center of the ego. We say there are nine basic styles or points of ego fixation. The easiest way for me to explain the fixations and the ideas that cure them is to use the diagrams, or enneagons, we have developed.

Let's take one ego type and see how this schema works. The

indolent type of person may be very energetic in his relations with the outside world but he does not take responsiblity for cultivating his essence. This fixation roots in an especially keen awareness of the absence of love and therefore of a sense of lacking being. The indolent type goes out looking for the love and meaning he feels deprived of; he becomes a continual seeker, but never a finder. This is his trap. He is always searching outside of himself for what can only be found within. But in a perverse way the seeker is ignorant about himself. He believes he knows all about other people and he doesn't hesitate to tell everyone else. The hell of the indolent is the worst of all the fixations because it leads to inner paralysis and indecision. The ego-indolent is always working very hard seeking, but until the last moment before the fixation breaks, he vacillates and never quite takes the responsibility for his own life. He is always dealing with the largest issues of identity and destiny—total truth and total perfection—but he feels how far he is from being able to love and act authentically. The indolent person frequently tries to use sex to gain love. He makes the whole world over into the image of the absent mother. *The Confessions of St. Augustine* is a good illustration of the inner world of the indolent type. Augustine remained a seeker until he allowed God to find him.

Q: The more you talk about the inner dynamics of this fixation the more it sounds like a description of the universal human condition. There is a void at the center of every psyche. You can call it the absent mother, nothingness, ontological anxiety, divine restlessness, or the unreasonable fear of death. But it seems to be characteristic of every person.

OSCAR: It is a fundamental condition of all ego consciousness, but some people are more aware of it than others. The indolent fixation is at the head of the enneagon because it focuses on the most universal aspect of the ego's deprivation. In the same way, the remedy for indolence is in some way the remedy which cures all egos—the idea of holy love.

Love starts in the moment a man contemplates the creation

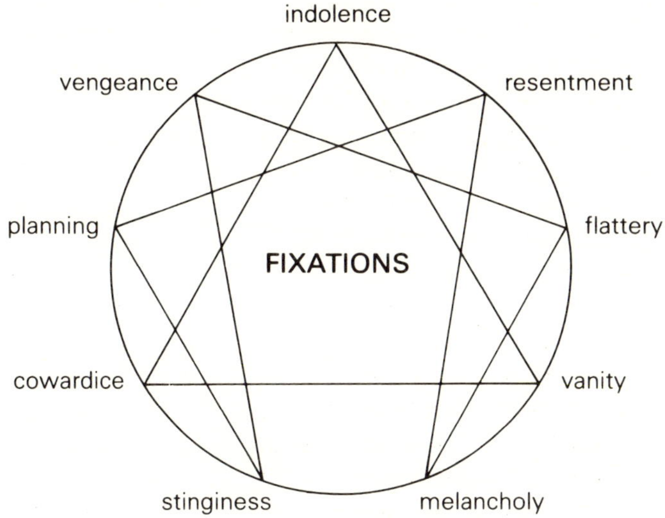

and says, "Thank You, God." The Holy Spirit really takes care of the universe; it is the active principle of love in all things. And it is only by getting in touch with this spirit that the indolence of the ego is transformed into active love. Holy love breaks the indolence and removes the feeling of separateness. With holy love comes the awareness that although the laws which govern reality are objective, they are not cold, because they lead to the creation of organic life that fulfills a cosmic purpose.

Q: I would like to go on a small tangent. Your theory of personality goes back to the traditional religious affirmation that man has no secure identity apart from the knowledge of his divine origin and destiny. Lacking knowledge of what Thomas Aquinas called the perfections of God, man tries to compensate. The various ego fixations are merely varieties of ignorance of the divine. Is psychic health possible apart from a religious view of the world? Can't we save the ego rather than get rid of it?

OSCAR: We have no desire to strengthen the ego or to make it happy. Short of enlightenment there is no way to harmonize and

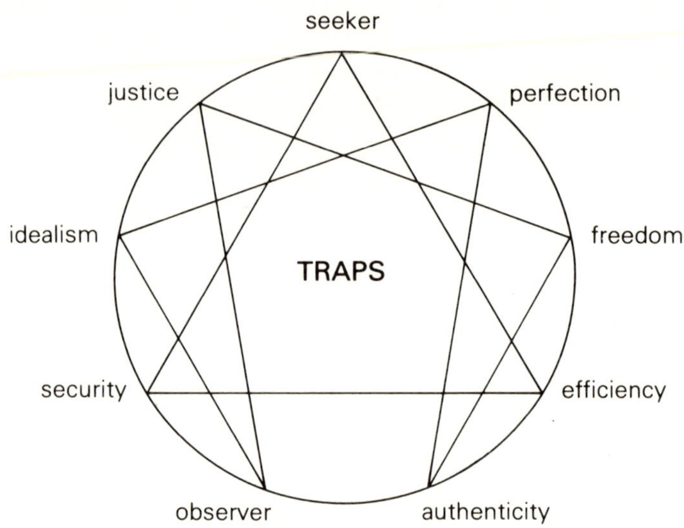
seeker
justice
perfection
idealism
freedom
TRAPS
security
efficiency
observer
authenticity

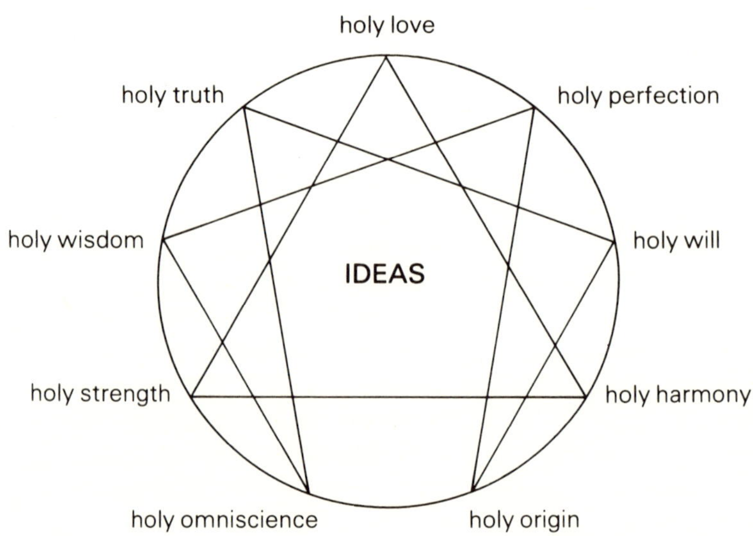
holy love
holy truth
holy perfection
holy wisdom
holy will
IDEAS
holy strength
holy harmony
holy omniscience
holy origin

unify the psyche. When man is in essence he knows he is within the divine unity. Only then does the dreadful alienation of the ego with all of its defensiveness and fear disappear. There is no peace short of being within the divine consciousness. It should be clear by now that the Western secular attempt to live without knowledge of the sacred unity of all things is a failure.

Q: Are you proposing a new religion? And is Arica a new church?

OSCAR: Not at all. The disciplines we teach are very old. Many of them are adapted from traditional Buddhist, Taoist, Islamic, or Christian sources. But we do not have any creed or dogma. We introduce people to techniques that facilitate experiences but we are experimental in our approach. We do not ask for any belief or faith. We only say: try these things and see what happens to you. But the group, the community, is an important part of the work. When people see others with their same ego fixation they feel less alone and less serious about their hang-ups. We do the work of ego reduction with a lot of humor and laughter. And all this helps. When a person feels a part of a community of fools or sinners he begins to realize that the pretensions of the ego are no longer necessary.

Q: It appears that you are grafting an Eastern understanding of the human condition onto a Western society. I wonder both how effective and salutary it will be. Western religion and psychology made an effort to free man from consciousness, from excessive introspection. Both Christianity and Freud defined maturity in terms of the ability to love and to work. Your trip seems to increase introspection to the point where it becomes a total preoccupation. Meditations, mantras and mudras seem to fill the day of the Arica student.

OSCAR: Any form of meditation or discipline to raise consciousness initially creates greater self-consciousness because the ego reacts with fear to the threat that it may die. But as the essence is nourished by the disciplines and the love within the group, ego consciousness is lost and there is a new awareness and appreciation of the world. Our aim is not to detach people

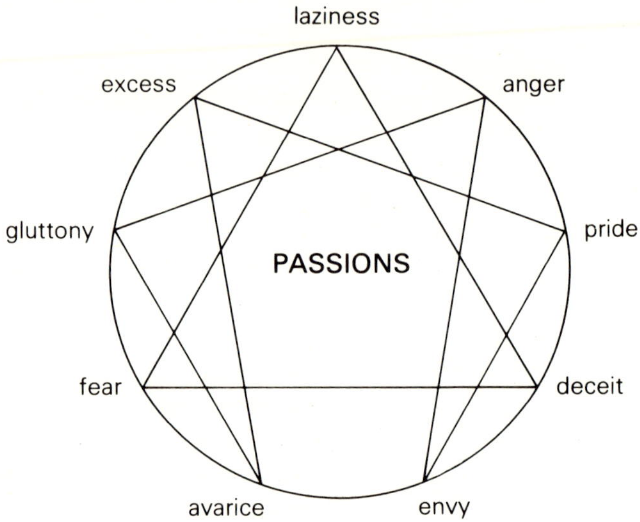
laziness
anger
pride
deceit
envy
avarice
fear
gluttony
excess
PASSIONS

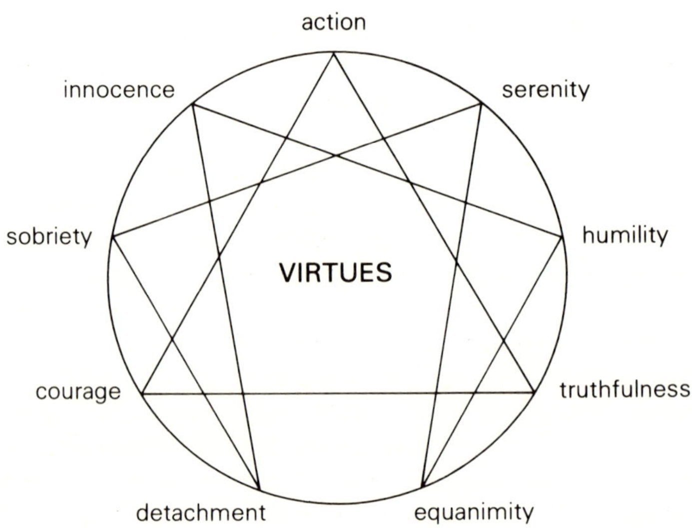
action
serenity
humility
truthfulness
equanimity
detachment
courage
sobriety
innocence
VIRTUES

from this world but to train them to change it—to slow down and love the earth—before it is too late.

Q: Let's get back to some of the other techniques for destroying the ego. How do you deal with the emotional component of the ego?

OSCAR: There are certain biological understandings within the body which naturally result in a harmonious emotional life. These are the objective virtues. An essential individual will be in contact with these constantly, simply by living in his body. But the subjective individual, the ego, loses touch with these virtues. Then the personality attempts to compensate by developing passions. The passions, which are a product of the mind alone, can be seen as the subjective expression of the lack of the objective virtues. Again, the fastest and clearest way to see the relation of these ideas is to use the enneagons.

Let's follow the example that we began earlier. The top place on the enneagon is the dominant passion for the indolent ego type—laziness. Laziness refers to avoidance of the work required to develop essence and it is a compensation for the lack of the virtue, action. True activity takes place when the body is healthy and receptive to energy from the kath. This can happen only when the head is empty—that is, in satori. Activity doesn't result from a command of the mind. You can go on around the points of the enneagon and do a comparable analysis for the other ego types.

We have many techniques for dealing with the emotional component of ego structure and we are always experimenting with new methods. Since fear is a defense mechanism of the ego connected with protecting an image of the self, we sometimes have people compile a long list of words that are insulting to them. Then we work with these until they have been emotionally neutralized. We also make use of mudras—body positions like the *asanas* in yoga—that create a disposition for the objective virtues. These are stances and gestures that give the feeling of courage or humility. An important part of our work is creating a sensitivity to different ways of breathing; shallow upper-chest breathing is typical of ego consciousness while kath breathing is more characteristic of the person who is in essence. We teach the art of creating rituals and ceremonies, liturgies for the new spiritual consciousness. And, of course, since many of our teachers are ex-Esalenists, we use many of the techniques of self-knowledge that have been developed in humanistic psychology.

Q: You have saved the best for last. How do we reach the state of blessedness when the mind is empty of chatter, defenses, plans, and games, and the kath is the master of life?

OSCAR: That is a little bit like asking, "What are your techniques for doing nothing?" When we are in perfect awareness we know nothing and we are immediately in the action of nonaction. It happens naturally. In China they called this *wu wei.* In Taoism nature moves you; you don't move it. All of our work is aimed toward this goal, but nothing we do makes it happen. When the ego is broken the essence quite naturally takes over. The collapse comes at the moment when the ego games are completely exposed and understood; illusion is shattered; subjectivity is destroyed; karma is burned.

Q: Perhaps the moment of grace cannot be programmed but you do have a whole technology for developing awareness of the kath.

OSCAR: Yes. The transfer of consciousness from head to kath is a constant emphasis of the Arica program, but the work with movement, breathing, and mantra focuses especially on this problem. We have a program of regular exercises that tone up the body and make it flexible. We use things like African dance, eurythmics, and drumming to develop kath awareness. The mantras and chants increase body awareness by training people to feel sound and vibrations in the various centers of the body. Probably the strongest and most ancient methods we use are the respiratory techniques.

What Eastern philosophers referred to as prana yoga we call alpha breathing. The same alpha frequencies that are in our brains are also in the ionosphere, so we can unite the psyche and the cosmos in the act of breathing. In ego breathing, the head controls by interrupting the natural flow. In natural breathing, we stop ordering the lungs and become receptive to the way the organism wants to breathe. In the moment when we let go, we realize that we do not have to make ourselves breathe: He is breathing us.

Q: The image of breath seems to be central to most religious traditions. Our words 'animal' and 'spirit' and 'inspiration' all go back to the root image of 'breathe'. In the Hebraic tradition man became man at the point when God breathed His spirit into him. More recently, psychology seems to have discovered what yoga practitioners have known for centuries—anxiety is always accompanied by interrupted respiration.

The consciousness revolution we are experiencing is in some way connected with the rediscovery of breathing. When we concentrate on breathing we see the paradox that we keep consciously interfering with a process that works perfectly naturally so long as it remains unconscious. Our split between doing and allowing, between conscious command of the whole of life and surrender to natural rhythms that are not of our making, is symbolically dramatized in our breathing. The age of anxiety is the age of over-controlled breath. The new spiritual revolution is animated by the hope of finding our way back to the power that breathes us, to the force that lives beneath the level of our conscious minds.

OSCAR: As a culture, our awareness is beginning to shift from ego to kath. The process of awakening in humanity is parallel to the process in an individual. We are no longer on an individual trip. The whole society is raising its consciousness. All history up to this point has been winter. Now spring is coming for sure. We are living in the time of the transformation.

Q: What evidence do you have that the consciousness revolution is a great awakening and not merely another fad?

OSCAR: The contradictions within Western culture have reached such massive proportions that we either must change or die. We are similar to the man who sees that his ego only produces greater conflict, competition, suspicion, and fear. The logic of technology is driving us faster and faster into a culture of perpetual change in which we are exhausting both our psyches and our natural resources. The way of life that creates a hunger in us for more and more, faster and faster, leaves us unsatisfied. The hope for both personal and cultural transformation lies in the fact that ego always ends up killing ego. When the velocity toward satisfying ego needs increases to a certain point, the whole ego system collapses; the absurdity and contradictions are suddenly obvious. This is the first satori. Our culture is now experiencing the first moment of enlightenment.

Q: There is another, less optimistic, way to interpret the consciousness revolution. It may be the sign of the death rather than the rebirth of our culture. The traditional Western dream was that we could know and control nature in sufficient degree to create "an alabaster city undimmed by human tears." But our ethic of work and our obsession with the technological dream have produced Vietnam, trips to the moon, and a hopelessness about fundamental political and social changes. There is no American dream. We seem to have lost our nerve. And so we are turning inward. If we can't change the exterior world we can at least change our consciousness. I sometimes think three million people a month read *Psychology Today* in hope of finding some succor for a lost something they used to call their souls.

OSCAR: That is a possible way of looking at things, but I think it is wrong. Too many forces are converging to make an awakening inevitable. Take the media, for instance; they are the nervous system of the culture. So now the nervous system is getting connected. Television and computers give us fast feedback from the extremities of our social organism to the central nervous system. We are becoming more sensitive. We see and feel what we are doing to ourselves with our insane velocity.

Q: But vision can be blinding. It may be, as Zorba said, that we are too damn sensitive. We may have immobilized ourselves with sensitivity. And the sign of this immobilization may be that the people who a couple of years ago were outraged enough to want to change the culture are now moving into the inner world. Jerry Rubin is reputed to have given up the politics of confrontation for bioenergetics. Many of my friends who were in the radical left are now more involved in body therapies—Rolfing, sensitivity, Reichian therapy—than in the body politic.

OSCAR: But even the paralysis may be a sign of the end of the old order. In the ego-indolent fixation, for instance, right before the ego breaks, there is tremendous exterior movement combined with interior paralysis. And also the cultural elite are already beyond the materialistic dream and are rediscovering the spiritual unity of the cosmos.

From a practical perspective we need a cosmic vision to create the ecological consciousness necessary to survive on this planet. The world is not limitlessness, so we must discover that humanity is one body. If the idea of reincarnation is real—and it is—then all the people who ever existed in the world are now alive. We all are now. Humanity is the Messiah and we are awakening to that fact. That is the meaning of the consciousness revolution.

Q: Maybe. Maybe. I wish I had your confidence. But I look at history and see too many times when we have been at similar points and there have been similar apocalyptic philosophies. Someone has always been proclaiming the end of the world, and the world to their embarrassment kept on its muddled, ambivalent way. Jesus and the Essenes read the signs of the times and saw the Kingdom of God approaching. So did Kant and Hegel and the thinkers of the Enlightenment. Visions of utopia, enlightenment, and the best of all possible worlds are dangerous because they make us discontent with the actual world and make coping seem like a compromise. When Kierkegaard said to Hegel, "I am only a limited existing human being. I cannot stand outside of my historical condition in order to see the unfolding of the Absolute Spirit," he was giving the existentialist warning against the visions of an idealist. Or, as a Buddhist tradition says: samsara is nirvana. This world of suffering is where we find happiness; it isn't the best of all possible worlds, it is only the best one we have. And the danger is that visions of the awakening of God become so easily politicized. Hegel saw the German State as the incarnation of the Absolute Spirit in history, and we see the American State as the defensive arm of the God in whom we trust to make the world safe for democracy. Whenever you have a utopian vision, there is always a grand inquisitor hidden in back of the scene pulling the strings to make things happen in the right and holy manner.

OSCAR: In past eras the mystical trip was an individual matter, or at least a matter of small groups, but no longer. This is what is new in human history. Everybody can now achieve a higher degree of consciousness. We can all take this trip together. True democracy is based on the fact that in essence we are all equal and perfect. So the idea of a leader for the new consciousness revolution is no longer necessary. It is more that humanity is an organic body that goes through the same stages an individual does on the path toward enlightenment. In Western culture competition has reached such a velocity that consciousness must inevitably change. When the ego or a society reaps the full hell they have sown in their quest for false security and status, they come to the point of collapse and rebirth. Already the new vision of the world is capturing the young people. Our minds are enlarging and our aims becoming more universal. The vision of humanity as one enormous family, one objective tribe, may once have been utopian. Now it is a practical necessity.

THE FIELD OF DECISIONS

Interview by Timothy Wilson, 1975

THE YEAR 1975 was a turning point in Arica. Beginning in the fall of 1974 with a school-wide conference to discuss the method of expansion, plans were developed for making the Arica theory and method available to the widest audience possible. As it happened, the great expansion that did take place was within the curriculum itself.

In an event of dramatic significance, the first yantra, the 'Birth of Light', was introduced to the School and was 'opened' with a series of four extended meditations or 'tunings', done simultaneously by Aricans throughout the world. The 'Birth of Light' meditation also introduced the mantra TOHAM KUM RAH. At the second tuning, on New Year's Day, a taped message from Oscar was read. In it he spoke of our time as the "sunset" of humanity's history, and he stressed that if humanity were to survive the coming crisis, the Arica system would have to appeal to the people of the working class. If not, then there was no hope of producing the giant wave of consciousness in society for which the School had been preparing itself.

Later in the year, Oscar gave a series of five lectures on the subjects of Mind, Reason, Consciousness, History, and the Arica system, subsequently published in *The Human Process for Enlightenment and Freedom* (Arica Institute, 1976). He also advanced many of the concepts that would carry the School through its next stage of development, concepts elaborated in this previously unpublished interview with Timothy Wilson.

In other talks that year Oscar announced that the School was complete. He likened its construction to the building of the great pyramids of Egypt which, he said, had also been built for internal development. The Arica pyramid, though a psychic rather than physical structure, had been difficult to build, requiring the sweat and effort of people who had to be one hundred percent committed to the School, pooling all their energy and creativity for this common goal. The time had now come, he said, for Aricans to take full responsibility for the School in a democratic process.

With the construction of the School finished, Oscar was now free to work on refining, clarifying, and publishing the Arica system in a series of training manuals.

The expansive mood of these times is clear in this interview. Oscar speaks candidly about a variety of topics ranging from his childhood to world history to the experience of divine revelation. A primary focus, however, is on the "field of decisions" where the game of history will be played out and decided by the strength of the working class. He stresses the importance of trialectics, the logic of the unity, as a critique of reason and Arica as the first major revision of Buddhism in 2,500 years, providing the science of realization for the next 2,500 years.

TIMOTHY WILSON: I'm afraid I don't know where to begin....

OSCAR ICHAZO: Most of the time the first question is: How did you start on this? How did it happen? And every time I try to answer, I find myself in the uncomfortable position of not being able to explain anything. When I was six and a half years old I started having certain kinds of experiences, or more than experiences, what I would call psychic realities. But the fact is that these experiences would not have happened if I had not been predisposed toward them somehow. Now, I don't know what happened to me, but I can say this: the first time I noticed in the church that there was the image of Jesus hanging there—dead, it was a very shocking thing.

Q: In the church?

OSCAR: In the church. My eyes opened. I was not precisely a devotee, but I was very careful to be punctual every Sunday and on certain holidays. That was all. Always I would pray. But what they said about colors and the saints and all that stuff had absolutely no significance for me, as I well recall. I was already in school. I had started in a Jesuit school where all the priests were Spanish, very Catholic, very old style. They were extremely rigorous with the Mass every day. Of course they gave the explanation that Jesus was dead and crucified. But the idea of a man hanging dead was too much for me. I can't explain why; it was just too much, so much that I couldn't get it out of my mind after that. Since that time I had been living in a kind of limbo—I wouldn't say a limbo of happiness because that kind of thing precisely does not exist in childhood. I had a very fortunate childhood because my mother really cared for my conservation very strongly. So that area was well cared for. But the preoccupations of the child are always his own preoccupations and his own process and his own health, whether there is care or no care. For me, though, my mother was quite a help.

I can remember from before I was one year old. I don't know why, but I remember things precisely. Those first years were unbelievably lucid for me. I remember hearing entire conversations of people talking. I used to be totally mute, silent. I wouldn't move from one place. At the beginning they were a little bit worried about me; they wondered why I didn't play and why I was so quiet. But then I started walking without crawling first. I just stood up and started walking. I was about eleven months old when I jumped up and started walking. But even though I could walk very well, I preferred just to stay sitting in one place without moving and watch. Why that? I don't know. For me that was something incredible. For example, if I had to be with my mother while she had tea with another senora, I would hear what they were talking about, and I could be sitting down for two, three hours and they would totally forget I was there because I was so involved with seeing the family and the characters there. One of my uncles was incredibly fat. I could never put my arms around him. I always went behind him because I wanted to measure him, but he was always bigger than my hands. He died when I was four years old.

And then there was that war between Paraguay and Bolivia. My father was very young, and during the war he made his career. He really didn't have anything else but his career; he was a self-made man with nothing behind him, really nothing. Otherwise he had a very good role. He went to the war as a captain and he came back as a colonel. But what I want to say here is that nobody was aware of me. I was a child. When I was a little bit bigger, I would sit in another room in the dark and listen to what the adults were talking about—politics and this and that, who had been killed. Now it's different, but in those times it used to be extraordinarily violent. Every two months you would have a revolution, and revolution will always disrupt your life. The game was like that.

Q: I wanted to ask you more about the culture now.

OSCAR: The most important thing to recognize is that for one reason or another historians have completely forgotten what causes a culture to be born. Perhaps they have not forgotten, but all of them have completely missed the point. The point is very simple. A culture is born only and exclusively when the unity of God is discovered.

For the Egyptians, Menes discovered the unity of God. The Egyptians discovered that a man can get into the divine state. They discovered that. We don't know their precise techniques because the Egyptian mysteries were exactly that, mysteries. They were not the only example of mysteries, but all the rest follow the same pattern. You have Menes and you have Egypt. You have the Vedas and you have all the Aryan culture. You have the Yellow Emperor and you have China. You have Lao Tzu later in China and again there is another China.

Now, the same is true with Moses; the same is true with Jesus. With Jesus a culture is born, the Christian culture. Ours is not a Roman culture and we are not a combination of the Greek, the Roman, and the Christian, as most historians say. Things are not like that anyhow. It depends on the cultural matrix and the cultural energy at the time, but it is always precipitated by the discovery of the unity of God. With Mohammed, again there is a discovery of the unity and another culture is born.

Of course Gautama is another proof. Padmasambhava in Tibet is another proof; when he went to Tibet a whole culture was born. Another example is the Sixth Patriarch in China. He just arrived and another culture was born inside of the already gigantic Chinese culture.

Now the problem is this, and I want to speak about this because it must be clarified. It has become very, let's say, fashionable to say that spirituality is scientific. Everyone claims for himself a spirituality that is scientific because, well, it's beautiful to claim that. Now, for instance, they say that tantra is science. I am astonished! They say that yoga is science; they say the Kaballah is science, the pure mystical science of the Kaballah! It's just ignorance to speak like that; there is no other word for it. It is just not knowing what science is, because science works with measurements. Tantra hasn't got them, yoga hasn't, nor has the Kaballah.

Now I would say this very concretely: nobody found the parameters before I did. Why? Because I have measured the psyche. I have the measurements. I know the parameters. I know there are nine domains, not one more, not one less, and that's it. I know that there are only four possible scales and no more: the scale of the psychotic, the scale of the subjective, the scale of realization, and the scale of man-God. That's all. There are no more. Inside that territory there is nothing that we don't know with total and complete precision because we know the measurements. *That's* science. Anyone who comes to me and says, "I'm scientific in spiritual matters," and doesn't show me parameters, is just speaking nonsense.

I am saying that a culture is born when the unity of God is discovered. We say in the Arica theory that these measurements are totally new things and that nobody else discovered them before. The theory says that human beings have a psychic process and all the psychic processes are alike. This is inevitable and nobody can avoid his process. You can pray all you want but your process is not going to be shortened by even one inch. Nevertheless, you can speed up the process. That can be done. We are the first to discover that, because we know the territory and we know there is a process.

Q: This is the first time this has come into the culture?

OSCAR: Of course. The first big discovery for our culture was Aristotle's discovery of the laws of logic. That is, that reason works under certain laws which are inevitable, and that there are just three laws and no more. You can try to find powerful reasons for anything, but it is inevitable that there are no more than three. Aristotle saw it perfectly, and reason was proved as logic. Before Aristotle, everything in Greece was becoming a sophism. Where was the truth? No more truth. Everything was relative, and if you talk well, that's enough; you don't have to mean anything. With Aristotle that was finished. And without his discovery this culture also would be impossible.

Q: After all these cultures and realizations, where are we now in the process?

OSCAR: You know, in the Orient they forget very easily that for us there is no contradiction between movement and life. We don't have contradiction with movement because with dialectics it has been proved that there is no contradiction with movement. It has been proved that movement is logical. That is dialectics: proving that movement is logical. But that means the process is endless, and the endless process doesn't exist. It is out of reality. So, if you see, with dialectics the process is demonstrated, no doubt, but since it is endless, it is lacking something very radical. So we come to trialectics. With trialectics we prove that not only is the unity explicable, but it is logical as well, and with that we really close the circle. We are demonstrating God by reason. This may look like nonsense because God has always been understood only by faith, never by reason. Now, what happened, mostly in the Orient, is this: they don't know how to reason well. They are not experts at logic; they are not experts at dialectics. Anyhow, those things exist and they work because they are laws. Trialectics is also laws. There is a law of mutation; there is a law of circulation; there is a law of attraction, and that's it. This is a discovery equal to the syllogisms of Aristotle, which is one of the most amazing things ever devised by a human mind. He includes all the possibilities of logic—there is nothing else; everything is included—and he tells you immediately which are the sophisms. It is certainly impressive, that work.

Now we are in a different level. We are proving the unity of God; we are proving the process, through which we are proving that man is not a coincidence. We are proving another thing also: that man is the top and the end and there is no more evolution. Evolution has finished with man. We say that, even though man is going to evolve inside himself naturally to a state that nobody dreams about. Now it is too far, but in another 2,500 years it is not going to be far.

The problems are like this. America was able to evolve because the conditions of the territory and the possibilities of expansion and of a free market enlarging almost endlessly have made this country exactly what it is, in a concrete and total dialectical process. That this has never been said—well, I'm sorry—but from the very beginning when this country started as a country, it's been a country just for competing. Competition is the basic thing that makes it dialectical because pure dialectics is based on contradiction, opposition, and competition.

Q: How does this manifest?

OSCAR: It manifests in a better creativity, in more activity and in an impulse that in time becomes second nature to you. I see you and I try to imitate you and be better. I am always in the state of trying to be better until it comes naturally. But Europe has been, let's say, the bastion of the logical culture, and it is strong because through war it evolved in all its power. The most logical of all the structures of the West, of Europe, is without any doubt the Catholic Church—it is absolutely ordered and absolutely Aristotelian. St. Thomas Aquinas was absolutely Aristotelian, one hundred percent. Now, this condition has made the logical structure of thought very heavy, particularly in the Catholic countries, and they have become stuck in the logical position more than the Nordic countries that have, let's say, gone farther toward the position of rapport that is already a principle of the dialectical position. Europe advanced to the dialectical position in what moment? In the moment of neutralization; that's when. But Europe must play politics all the time because its history has been one giant country against another giant country, and the competition was between countries rather than internal. In Europe they didn't need internal competition; they have enough externally to go on and on endlessly.

Here in America the competition was established more from man to man. In Europe the competition was structured more between nations or groups or parts of groups. Now that is of course not only dissolving but also evolving; we don't know how much and with what unbelievable speed. That is precisely the explosive thing for me. I find the advantage there, in Europe, because once that goes, it really goes.

But speaking about America: basically this is a dialectical society based on competition and contradiction in an endless figure. That's why encountering limits comes as such a surprise now. The world is just not that big. Nobody can claim ownership, very obviously not. This is a shocking surprise for Americans because everything here was planned for endless millennia of happiness and what do you know? It didn't even go for ten years. It works out splendidly, because undoubtedly that is not now the American position. In America if somebody is still in that position, he hasn't read the news. It is obvious also that interdependence becomes necessary with this matter of the oil. Just take the light bulbs out in this country and we will all start screaming. It is unbelievable. But, you know, everything says that we are going to the unity in one way or another. The planet is not that big. But all those are pretty good reasons.

Q: What is saying that we are going to the unity?

OSCAR: The only thing that can get to the unity is the unity itself. Now the recognition of what a human being is comes only when he achieves the state and knows that he is TOHAM KUM RAH, and that's it, because that is the word, the first—meaning that with that all the universe has been created—that is Alpha—and it is going to finish in the same TOHAM KUM RAH—that is Omega. So the saying that a man is a microcosm is completely true. Now I am speaking scientifically, so you know the thing is this way. Number one: the most important thing for American society as a whole, and especially for the youth of America, is concretely and specifically to become aware of what man is, and what each individual is. There is, of course, a tremendous natural inclination for that. America really is filled with seekers, and every year there is a kind of proliferation. In a few years the mentality has changed so deeply that it's really something to see.

Q: What precisely is that change of mentality?

OSCAR: The change of mentality has come, number one, with LSD, a very dangerous drug, as we know. If you are not an expert in it, it's almost better not to take it. But it did have the impact of a physical discovery of the spirit. I say 'physical discovery', but it's more of a chemical discovery. That has been one change.

Another thing has been that precisely with the understanding of the drugs, America suddenly became aware that there was a kind of sacred knowledge in almost every culture and that the Indian cultures, at any rate, have got their own thing. That was very important. In the midst of this, because without it it wouldn't be possible, comes Castaneda's fake. I say it like that because it is a fake! But that's another matter. There are other things more important than that.

Another very big discovery, amazingly enough at first glance, has been the discovery of kung fu. Of course that has not really been discovered; it has been popularized. But do you know why

I say it was important? Because of this: martial arts in any degree, however they come, are extraordinary pacifiers. The man who has attained any position in martial arts becomes a very peaceful man after that. This is a common experience. It is the experience that aggression goes away first during the training; all one's aggressiveness is going to go away. That's one. Number two is that you see that the thing is so violent that it would be better not to try it; you will always be aware that perhaps there is somebody who knows it better and could hurt you badly. It is a tranquilizer which defuses the explosive part of you because you see you can no longer afford to be explosive. Before, you could have combat with your fists, enormous combat with fists. Now with karate thinking you see that fists can't do it; you would lose too much blood. You can't, because it is just a different thing. So the first view is of a shocking and violent thing, and the second view is a tremendous pacifier.

Another thing of major importance to American society, of shocking importance really, was Vietnam. I say shocking because we found that a little country is not that easy to beat. It had such a tremendous power. It's astonishing what man can do if he really wants to, whatever his project. This marks a return of respect for human beings, because for a while we were totally in love with machines. Now Vietnam has proved one thing: society will always be equal to the strength of its individuals rather than the strength of its machines, and its individuals will always be strong if they are united by a common idea. Anyhow, we are not discussing what the ideals are here. Let us just see the pattern, the whole pattern. Another very obvious thing is that the shortage of oil has changed our mentality very strongly, just by way of example.

Q: How has the oil crisis changed the mentality?

OSCAR: Only in the sense that now there is a dependence. We can't make our own terms just because we are stronger. The idea that being the strongest doesn't guarantee that you can do anything you want is also a shocking thing.

Q: What direction is society moving in now?

OSCAR: Another factor that now comes into the picture is the realization that the energy of the labor force must be deeply understood. I'm just pointing out a direction because it is inevitable. It is inevitable because the entire society is in the process of change. But we know perfectly well that if labor doesn't make the change, none of the rest will. That's definite. Here I'm speaking scientifically. I know. I am not voicing an opinion. Normally this society has a big advantage. It has the advantage of being extraordinarily sensitive to its internal problems, extraordinarily sensitive. Because of that and because there are a lot of upwardly mobile people with freedom for their movement, the painful areas are usually detected very soon. Another thing is that here we have a free media that has now become unbelievably encouraged and courageous in the sense that they have lost respect for anything and will go and smell out any story. I am speaking about Watergate and other things which have made tremendously important changes. Watergate meant the end of the unlimited power of the executive. With that, the press has now risen to a position of enormous strength in the country. Never before have we had the kind of press we have now. They are so direct it's almost shocking, and of course now that's the game and everybody is playing it. Again it is the competition working. A media that has achieved this degree of strength of course makes this organism very sensitive. So the area that is going to be detected as an area of urgent importance is the necessity of involving the labor energies in the entire game, knowing that if the labor energies go into the game, we all go. So let's say it is good business and is the shortest way.

Now counting all these together, they are facts that in reality are questions that this society is answering one after the other. Because Vietnam and all the rest brought up the question, What are we doing? And the next question, All this for what? Now when you go to that point, you are extraordinarily close to the Buddhic questions that are inside all of us. Gautama just discovered them, but they are inside all of us all the time. Where do I come from? Who am I? Where am I going? But, you know, that 'Who am I?' is finally going to be the achievement of this society. The achievement of this society is going to be the recognition of the quality of a human being under the best possible conditions and trying to imagine what those best possible conditions are, knowing that this information must immediately be transmitted to all the rest because that's the business. We can't say we are at that point yet, but that does indicate the direction.

Q: What is required for us to get to that point?

OSCAR: The energy comes first and always from the sacred mantra of a human being: TOHAM KUM RAH. That's not only basic, it's fundamental because it is the 'recalling'. With that recalling also is the recalling of your internal freedom that is tied to nothing, complete and total freedom. Now what we do is say, "This is the thing. It's a process and you can do it scientifically with measurements and in a concrete form if you want it that way. If you don't want it that way, that's also okay. You have your process and you know what to do about it. It is your own process and if you don't want to accelerate your process, that's part of your process also. There is no contradiction at all . . . ." But we are going to start saying, "The thing is just like this."

Q: There is only one way?

OSCAR: There is only one reality. Now, knowing the parameters, I don't say we want to be exclusive. We are not going to be like that. You know, once a law is discovered, the law is the same here or in China or Russia or anywhere. It is exactly the same. I don't mean this in the sense that we are unique as a group, because we're not. Without any awareness on our part, perhaps someone, who knows where, would start doing the same thing, and it would have the same effect. The method of Arica is independent of individuals because it is scientific. We say that tantra is not scientific, but why is it not scientific? Because there are no measurements. I'm not saying it's not precise; it is extraordinarily precise, but it's not scientific. As you know, the fisherman gets his fish; he is very practical, very technical, but he is certainly not scientific.

Q: What then is TOHAM KUM RAH?

OSCAR: TOHAM KUM RAH is the sacred divine internal name of a human being. Saying that is also saying this: it is the internal name of humanity as a whole, or we can say it is the name of the third person of the Trinity and is the way to become that. For us there is nothing higher than the mantra. So we are the first to take it to others, precisely because we know that. You have seen what has happened in San Francisco. All the time, people just go into the Rainbow Pyramid and they start saying TOHAM KUM RAH, and they change right there, of course. I would say it is inevitable.

Q: Are there any necessary preparatory steps to saying the mantra?

OSCAR: Only this one: to have a school. More than that, I would say two things: to have a school, without a doubt, and to have the theory complete and published. The theory of Arica is fundamentally a critique of reason as a whole. I'm not speaking here only in a Kantian way; I'm really speaking of the entire business, the whole thing. But there is a problem. Once this is discovered, the building of the School is accomplished. It has taken exactly five years to do it, really to achieve it, no less. This is fantastic, because somehow I knew with precision that it was going to take five years, and I told the Chile group it's going to be five years, but in me it was an internal calculus. I'm just amazed how precise it has become. It's the first of July again; it's five years, and the thing is finished.

Q: What do you mean when you say, "The School is finished"?

OSCAR: To finish is to have the first group of realized men with these techniques. These people had to go through the entire process and they had to understand cautiously all of the ancient ways because they were going to get a new one that was extraordinarily potent, by far more potent than all the rest. I know all the rest with precision, so I know exactly what I am talking about. Knowing that, I wouldn't just give them the new method from the first moment, or I wouldn't have the School; we wouldn't have the School; the School would just be blown away. We had to do this process because it is the incarnation of humanity as a whole. If you don't see that, you don't get the point of view you need for understanding this material.

The Aricans here are extraordinary in that they really can understand another culture with unbelievable ease, which is not very common in the United States. Why? Because the American has become absolutely absorbed by his internal process, so absorbed that that's almost enough for him. As the European knows from the very beginning, he has to look elsewhere to understand other cultures and other possibilities. Americans used to lack that kind of understanding, but now, after so many young people have gone to India and the Orient, all that has changed. But that outlook in the Aricans is different, absolutely guaranteed, because not only do they have the experience of having traveled a lot, but all of them also did the path. Arica is really the place for seekers, all of the first quality; otherwise they wouldn't have been able to do it; they just wouldn't do it. It has been extraordinarily heavy. Now why that heaviness? It's something else to consider. We had negativity all the time. To my way of thinking, I say, "Thank you," of course; it made the going easier rather than more difficult, amazing as that seems at first glance. But really, it is exactly like that. Why? Because most people don't have the patience to take the necessary time to be well-informed.

In another way Arica has been sustained during these five years only by a certain number of people, those who were one hundred percent committed. Now, before Arica, all of them were already seekers who went to the top, to the end where there was no more going. It is like when you reach the ocean and can't go any farther, you see? So these people had the tremendous advantage of having already been in too many trips of all kinds: drugs, psychotherapy, and all the kinds of things that were around Esalen. At that time Esalen was extraordinarily powerful and extraordinarily serious because the Tibetans were already there; there were proven Zen masters; Rolfing was around. These are things that really count in this culture, that really counted and still count. They discovered a large part of Sufism and a lot of other things. Esalen really played an incredible role.

Having all that, the history of Arica is so beautiful because we have this group of people, no doubt of the very, very, very strongest, undoubtedly of the top calibre, who came and started doing the School. If they hadn't been already practiced in all these kinds of things, it would have been almost impossible to do it; it would have been incomprehensible to them. But you know, I counted on only one thing all that time, the same as what I have counted on in myself all my life; the curiosity inside me was always, always, always what overcame me; I couldn't stop myself from trying to reach and study, even when I knew it was endless. It was really nuts but I still couldn't stop it. Now, that was not produced by anything outside. I know it is in human nature and in certain people. It is there in the seekers. If the seeker is real, he is going to wait and wait or whatever he has to do to get to the top, and he is going to do it.

I counted on that, not in a cold way, no, but with the certain knowledge from my own experience that such people exist. And I said to them at the beginning, "We are going to try the incredible. We are going to try to be one. We are going to try to go so far that we eliminate all that is known as the human contradiction. We are going so far, we are going to crystallize our consciousness so much that we will be so alike that we will really be one." And when that happens, the potential of the human psyche is so unbelievable that you can't express it in words. It's just so unbelievable it can do almost anything.

But you know, these things are just as I am saying; they are not any other way. If there is going to be a new humanity, it's going to be under specific conditions. There is no other way but that way if we want to count for the whole. I am not denying the ancient paths. They do their work, without any doubt. I'm just pointing out that there is another method available, this time scientific. This is the first time we have something scientific because we have the complete measurement. That's why.

Q: Now that the internal process of the School has been completed, what is its mission to humanity? And what is the energy in humanity right now that will enable it to realize itself?

OSCAR: You see, first of all, we don't proselytize because it's obvious. You don't do proselytism with science. I don't see anybody beating a drum in the street and saying, "Gravitation is the beautiful thing and it's so and so." It doesn't make sense. This is equal to that. So we don't need to proselytize; it's not the game. You proselytize when you are working on the basis of faith. We are not working on the basis of faith. We are working on the basis of reason, because we have discovered a way of reason that leads us to the unity. We have discovered all the forces inside the human psyche. We know that the psychic space is just as we say. There is no other way. Because somebody is six feet five or six feet eight or whatever, he is not going to have a bigger pyramid—no, no, no—these are objective measurements. That is connected with all of gravitation, a problem I am going to speak about in the book I am writing. I am leaving that problem for later.

Q: What is happening in humanity now to bring it to this point of realization?

OSCAR: First, naturally, just the reality, the circumstances. Now, I am not going to believe for one second that the entire planet thinks the same way. The differences in the way we think now are very big and very strong.

Q: There are so many spiritual disciplines today. What is it that people can find in Arica?

OSCAR: The difference between Arica and all the rest is this: Mysticism in all the ancient ways, including the most practical, requires a certain amount of faith. Being practical, as we saw before, is not the same as being scientific. Practice and skill are one thing, not to be confused with science, which is fundamentally and basically measurements, quantification, parameters, and analysis of phenomena over those parameters.

Not every analysis of a phenomenon is science. A fisherman has to analyze phenomena, but that doesn't make him a scientist. But an oceanographer, yes, is a scientist because he is measuring the ocean and whatever life is there. That's science. Now, we say that Arica is the first scientific mysticism because we are the first to know those parameters. We can really act scientifically using measurements, establishing a territory, speaking of universal laws, proving that every psyche is alike, proving that a human psyche is not endless. Freud, Jung, all the psychologists up to this point believed in an unlimited psyche that was a frightened ghost. Well, there is no such frightened ghost, and even though the territory is quite large, it is nevertheless possible to really know the whole thing. A human life is designed, so to speak, precisely to fulfill all of its capacity and all the capability of its psyche, but it is not unlimited.

In ancient times, say two thousand years ago, if you wanted to go to the state of realization, you would only have faith for making the leap and it would have to be a lot of faith, otherwise you wouldn't do it. So the few that did it, once they went to the other side, when they were in the state of the divinized human being, were so far from the rest of the people that there was no link possible but the link of the guru with his disciples. And the disciples had to work years and years and years, imitating, imitating, imitating until perhaps in some moment they too could make the leap. And you never knew when the jump was going to happen, because it depended on your process. We know, so it's not a matter of knowing a secret, not a matter of a pure formula. It is a matter of work, but we know how to do it, and they didn't know how. The only way for them to do it was an artistic way of imitation. The better the imitation, the closer you were to doing the same. But of course, it was not guaranteed at all. That's the way art is. It's not guaranteed. We do guarantee. That's another difference, a radical difference. We *do* guarantee.

Q: What about the people outside the School? How can they make the jump? Or is it only in the School that this process takes place?

OSCAR: Without Arica there wouldn't be enough time to do it. What is Arica? Arica is more or less the vanguard of a thing that just has to happen. It is inevitable, because it certainly is the formula. So it's something that has to happen, as it had to happen that logic would be discovered, as it had to happen that dialectics would be discovered, as it had to happen that trialectics would be discovered, because these things are realities. They are so real that you can't change them. You know, there's another thing that has to stop—people think that they can make whatever they want with their mind. That's not so. There are laws, as there are laws for objects. There is gravitation and that's that. In the human psyche also there are laws that are laws. That means that it is radically impossible to avoid or to defy them.

Now the difference between a man who achieves his realization scientifically and a man who makes his realization, let's say, artistically, is enormous. It is a big difference. It is even possible to say that there is going to be a difference of intensity. With a scientific approach you can immediately think in terms of perfection, because you have the calculus of that process, you have a map of your process. The man who does his realization artistically does not even know what it was that made the jump happen, and it would be difficult to duplicate his experience with other people. When we proceed scientifically though, with maps and measurements, many people can work toward their realization at the same time with complete precision.

One thing is certain. If you want to speak of competition in this sense, who is going to be better? The one who achieves his realization scientifically. The only thing is that when he achieves that, he loses his desire to compete, because in that state competition just doesn't make sense. But do you think he has lost something? Not at all. He has won enormously. He has just lost the anxiety of the competition. And for what? For being transformed into total awareness: realistic, complete, secure, full of emotions, but true emotions, full of life, entirely happy, happy in the sense of having no extra emotional charge.

Although there can always be difficult tasks, that will have nothing to do with the internal happiness of knowing you have achieved what it is necessary to achieve as a human being.

You know, when you finally know the end of your psyche because you have already gone inside the training of dying, then there is no more fear. This is absolutely necessary. It is not a training of visualization; it's more than that; you really die. You have to go out of the body, but when you go out of the body, nothing happens. This time it's an exercise in which you are going to feel actually dying; you are actually going to feel how your senses go out one by one until the moment when there is only the last: consciousness. Then you realize exactly what the *bardo* is, and you do the bardo: that is, you die beforehand. Then there is no more fear; you can face death perfectly. That is another important thing because again it transforms consciousness tremendously, giving you an incredible love of life and a different sort of gratitude for being alive. Of course you can always repeat the experience again. But it makes a very peaceful man, though he is very strong, precisely because he has faced death and is not afraid.

Q: Is this a training that will be done?

OSCAR: That's in the monastery. It has to be in the monastery. It's the top.

Q: Are we moving toward a metasociety where we will all be one?

OSCAR: Yes, absolutely. You know, in this movement the task is going to be in the shape of a tripod, so to speak: one part is the United States, another is Europe, and the third, without any doubt, is the Soviet Union. There are two other extraordinarily big and complex countries: that is, China and Japan, but at the present moment they don't motorize, meaning they can't move the rest. China somehow is isolated with its internal problems, and it has a lot. Japan makes a very fair balance in the East and of course is basic for the balance of the whole world, but circumstances are such that it is not in the position to make the first move. Even though Japan could be more strongly advanced than all the rest here and there, I am speaking of something else, of being able to make a move that would have immediate repercussions in the whole rest of the world. So we can isolate these three points—Russia, Europe, and the USA—and see how in this very moment the entire game is being replayed in Europe; the entire game is there again. It's amazing to see how history returns to that point time and again where the game is being played. Now the Russians are so aware of that that it's unbelievable.

Q: What is the function of this tripod?

OSCAR: The problem is that in this balance, in the point where we are now, it seems almost like a matter of belief, a matter of choosing to believe in either capitalism or socialism. In reality there is no such choice because we've got to go to the third system, which is an entirely different thing, another MMP (material manifestation point) that has nothing to do with either one. In reality it is like that.

Q: Are you talking here about the democratic and socialist systems of America and Russia?

OSCAR: Let's say it's the socialist system versus the free society. Each has something to offer. In reality we are dealing with a *human* dichotomy. One side claims absolute and total right for the individual; the other claims absolute and total right for the community. But in this game there is a field of decisions that sooner or later will have to be made, because it is a balance and Europe is in the middle. Now the thing that makes Europe balance the other two nicely is that the consciousness of the labor strength there is enormously deep. I'm not saying 'strong', I'm saying 'deep', meaning really old and with a lot of experience. For some reason or other the labor force in Europe has been manipulated from one side to the other and back again, and all the manipulations have already been done. With that you have a process that has been completed, so you have people who are already different and who are just ready to make the incredible leap that is needed. But because society in general, and the European labor force in particular, has always had to submit to the national interest—always there is a war going on here or there—all the industry and everything gears up to start working, and the one who is always forgotten is the man who put his own strength in and made it move in the first place. This happens not so much because of the internal mechanisms of the countries as it does because of what we were speaking of before, the competition between countries in Europe. What goes on in the United States between General Motors and Ford goes on in Europe between Germany and France and England. That's just how it is. Now they have the common market and all that, but it wasn't always like that. History shows some major wars because of this competition in Europe. That you know.

So the labor force has suffered a particular denial, of which no one is guilty but the game itself. But this denial has acted like the pushing down of a coiled spring that can only be compressed so far before the mechanism is triggered and the spring recoils with the full force of its expansion. We are almost at that point. When that expansion comes—and lately I've been seeing this very clearly—it is going to be a rising of consciousness with an extraordinary human evaluation of where we are and what we want to do, one with tremendous talent and tremendous maturity. That maturity can really make the jump because, let's say, it can cure karma. When this moment comes, the only thing that can really be said is, "Goodbye to the past and thank you." We have learned that exceedingly well. There is a new man coming in Europe, coming from its strength, its labor forces, a man of incredible quality. This is why they will decide the game. For one thing the national interest is not that heavy now, so you no longer have those barriers that force working people into the position of denial where they submerge their own interest. There is no urgent national interest at present. That's one.

Another thing is that one way or another when the national interest needs the working people, the working people always do their job, but when the crisis of national interest is over, everybody forgets the ones who made the effort. It's a matter of circumstance and the situations of these countries. For now, those tensions are gone. In this very moment I don't suppose France is getting ready to bomb Germany or anything like that. I don't any longer see nationalistic wars in Europe.

Q: What do you see as the rise of labor?

OSCAR: Exactly that. For the first time the working people—the working energy, the basic energy—will decide the game. If the labor force is good for defending the national interest, it is also important as an international energy. That was very clear to Marx, but his criteria for this international strength of the labor force are fundamentally based on a common suffering, and it is not like that. Marx was wrong about that, no doubt. The solidarity exists, of course, but the root is different. What makes this solidarity, this basic solidarity? It is a very human thing: the working people know that their work is the same. In other areas you can imagine that it's not the same. For example, suppose we say that the pianists of Switzerland are exceptionally good and nobody else can match them because they are Swiss. In areas of art and that sort of thing you can have those kinds of claims. We don't know if they are real or not, but they are claims. However, about what is real energy you can't make claims; it is this much and that's it. Now, that strength is what keeps everything alive, and there is also the basic knowledge that it is like that. It's just a matter of realization; all the rest is there. It's also a matter of some more time, not much.

Q: Are the realizations that have to and are already taking place in the culture possible without the tools that Arica offers?

OSCAR: It is strange, as I am going to say. No. Radically not. However, I have to say this: if we wouldn't do it, somebody else would. This is inevitable. It happens that it is Arica that is doing it; it just happened to be Arica. But Arica is fundamentally a historic movement. That's another thing that makes Arica entirely different from all the rest; we are a historical movement. Why are we a historical movement? Because we have found the unity again upon a different basis, on the basis of reason, and we have found the unity to be scientific. That means a radically new mathematics, by the way; that means relativity is out. It means that we must go to the understanding of what the universe is; we must understand what gravity is and really disprove once and for all the nonsense about the attractions of one body to another.

Newton was a genius who really said, *supposing* that a mass attracts another mass, but that 'supposing' has been forgotten by everybody, especially the scientists. For them it's a dogma. Who said "So there exists an attraction between the sun and the earth"? There are some things I cannot understand. It almost makes you wonder what is in the mind of human beings. It's crazy. They look, they don't find anything of the kind in the entire universe, and still they continue to publish this nonsense.

Q: What is the historical process that started with Arica, and what is this new awareness that is essential to the culture?

OSCAR: From the moment that the School came to Arica and started the training—it was exactly that point—there was nothing else. I knew that the people who were coming to work with me had to be people who were already surrounded with their hands up because there was nothing else to do; they couldn't see any alternative.

Of course, one needed people of tremendous experience to be there. The amazing thing was that some of them in that group were so young; you couldn't believe they could be so young and still be in such an incredibly specialized thing. But you know, we insist that the truth doesn't need anything but itself because the truth is not supported by anything else but itself. If Arica is the truth, it is going to do it. How? We don't know. It is just going to do it.

In another way I have strong premonitions that have come to me in visions and from my life experience. For some reason or other I have always been so preoccupied with the movement of the thing, and I have felt the pain of what's coming here or there so acutely, and I don't know why. Perhaps everyone has his craziness, and this is mine. I want to say very concretely, though, that it is the experience of my entire life that gives me my vision, the vision I have now. At this point it is this concrete: I can almost see accurately what is coming just by using analogy, just by knowing what human beings really are, by really, really knowing what life is, by knowing with certainty what evolution is and where we are, by knowing with certainty what the universe is and where I am. That I can say just like that. Now with this volume of knowledge, we can make a new start. It's not that we *can* make a new start, we *have* to, we absolutely have to. If a solution doesn't come at the right time, it would be very dangerous, because in the moment of panic there is no control. That's human history; we know that.

Q: What is the truth that has to be communicated to mankind now?

OSCAR: First of all, of course, that humanity is one, that it is one spirit. We don't mean a superficial unity. Humanity is one body. Now every part of that body is of equal importance because this is an organism and in an organism there is no one thing more important than another. Going to an analogy, we can see that some points are more vital than others. But I want a better analogy. Here every part of what I am describing has to be considered absolutely necessary for all the rest, because it is like that. We are not aware that this spirit has been growing up; we are not aware that this body has been taking his own time, that it has not yet attained its full size. We have the population explosion to be concerned about, but what we mean by our size is not what people think; it's a little bit different; it's a different size. We didn't achieve this size yet. Now of course, the way things are going it's going to be very easy to do that. This population explosion is incredible, but the size is going to control itself if we last until then, because there are other problems; even though the problem of population size and the population explosion are extraordinarily dangerous, all that is not important at this point; there are more important things.

Q: What are they?

OSCAR: Some imbalance that can bring on the tragedy of war. That's something we don't want to think about now—nobody wants to—but that's not real, because in the position where things are now, with the contradictions that are present, there is no understanding. I am not going to believe that there is not enormous goodwill in the Soviet Union and here in America. Of course, it's obvious there is absolute goodwill. But things are not a matter of goodwill if there is no understanding. So long as the socialists maintain their position that only socialism works, we're going to have a hell of a contradiction.

Q: So what do we have to understand right now?

OSCAR: Right now we must understand absolutely that humanity is one. From that realization our moral point of view simply changes. So the second point is that we must not be so attached to our own particular societies or countries or whatever, that we become more universal and understand that the entire planet belongs to us. Of course the planet belongs to us but that's not really the point. We cannot go wherever we want; we cannot do enormous numbers of things because human beings are still tied to economic situations. Now we know that this can be overcome because we have the tools.

Let me repeat these points I mentioned: number one is that humanity is one spirit. How do you know that? You can have scientific proof, totally scientific. Our genes are the same in all human beings, and the proof is that it is possible to have intercourse with another human being from any culture and to produce a child that is identical in the sense that he can also continue this generation.

What makes that awareness so absolutely certain on a higher level is that the same divine name works exactly the same in everybody. Now that is not mental truth, it's not kath truth, it is *total* truth, because your heart feels it, your nerves feel it, your bones feel it; you really go inside TOHAM KUM RAH and you feel the entire humanity with a power that is just undeniable, the power of reality—and this is a divine reality—it is God-made. Those are the fundamental points.

Another point is the discovery of unity by way of reason, by way of logical reasoning. Speaking more precisely, it is not formal logic; it is trialectical logic. Why is this so important?

Because proving the unity of God with trialectical logic means it is possible to understand all that is inside the universe. That is why I speak about complete mathematics and not the mathematics of relativity.

Q: Will that proof be done? Has it been done?

OSCAR: Oh yes. Absolutely. It is just a matter of putting it on paper. I have done it already so many times that I know it by memory. But it is more than that, you know. I am desperate to do it, but everything has its time, and I will wait patiently for the time to do that. It is the last touch, and so it is going to come with crystalline clarity.

Why is this so important? Because then I can pass the absolute mathematics entirely and with perfection. But you know this is possible because we have a school. That is one thing we must understand. We have the three things that really make a reality. We have a school, we have a true teaching, scientifically speaking, and we have a true message that only comes by way of divine revelation. By a scientific approach alone I would never hear any further words. That's secure. Now the things that are revealed and the things that are discovered here are not exactly the same. When you go inside what revelation is and how it works, there is really a very precise way to do it. You know, in the movies when they try to imagine the position, suppose, of Moses and how he was, with that fire and all that—when you see how they represent it in the pictures, it's so far, so far from the truth.

Q: What is the experience of revelation?

OSCAR: This is really going to the nature of the experience. You know, when you face God, not as your own consciousness, which it is, but as a 'universal consciousness' consenting to you as a separate force, you become the subject of this presence that manifests as exterior to you, though in reality it's not exterior. It seems that you speak with someone, though it is not precisely speaking. Afterwards perhaps you want to transmit it to somebody, so you are going to try to put in words what was not spoken, because there are no words, even though it is a total and complete communication. The power of the light and how you see it really can't be explained. It's unbelievably raw, so to speak. But the popular understanding of what it is is so poor it's hilarious, enormously hilarious. I comment on this because I see that on TV they are doing Moses. Have you seen it? You didn't miss anything but the hilarious part. You did miss a very hilarious comedy. Anyhow, better this Moses than the other one of De Mille, much better. This Moses is a little bit more human; Burt Lancaster makes him more human. Nevertheless, they get into some points. One of them is that if a man is going to go into those states, it is not like they show in the movies where you beat your chest and go, "Oh oh oh wooh!" That's for a nut.

In reality you get really terrified and you don't know where you are going to put your head, because it is so uncomfortable. It is mostly uncomfortable because you can't really transmit the experience and yet you want to speak about it. That's only one part of the discomfort. What also makes the thing uncomfortable is that you know that you *have* to transmit it, and you don't know how to do it, and so you start the fight inside of you. I'll do it, I won't do it, I do it, I want to do it; and you fail and you fail again, and still you have that internal thing that says, "You have to do it." It's like once you have that experience, you have to transmit it, it's undeniable; you can do whatever you want but you always come back to the same point.

Q: How did you find a way of communicating?

OSCAR: I found a science. When it first came to me I wondered, "How am I going to do it?" I started to imagine how to do it, then I started saying, "I must see all the questions." I was not any longer in the state of divine coma—I have many, many experiences, but one, of course, of the most radical of all was that seven days of coma which came after really tremendous training. The idea of making trainings is Arica thought. I imagined that. Now why did I imagine that? For the simple reason that I could see the entire process, how it could be shortened and how we could use these laws and use speed like this and like that.

It happened to me like this. You know, I am not speaking of things I imagined. I am speaking of things I know. I was there not one time, but many times; that undoubtedly made me an expert in that field.

The problem with coming outside is that, okay, if there's going to be the truth, we've got to answer these questions:

What is a human being? What is life? What is evolution? What is gravity? What is the universe? What is matter? We don't have answers for all that. What's reason? What's truth? What's sex? I started with the questions and there were only questions and no answers.

I was certain before this experience that we were very far from the answers. But I was not concerned with them. I would see the problems just like that, and laugh a lot and be happy. In those times I was very happy in the sense of not having any responsibility. But with the responsibility came the fact that I started knowing that I had to discover the answers, and I started really working just for that.

You know, there is the tradition—and more than a tradition, it's a real fact—that every 2,500 years we have a change. The first to say that was the holy Gautama, and he was speaking about the tradition of the Buddhas in mankind. Gautama was the number three Buddha. 2,500 years before him there was one, and 2,500 years before that was another. Gautama spoke directly of the next 2,500 years, and it is in the tradition of Buddhism that in another 2,500 years we are going to achieve the perfect state as humanity. That perfect state is called *Maitreya.* Maitreya is going first to incarnate in somebody and then just spread. But in a way Maitreya has two roles. It has a first role and a second role and that makes for a confusion, because in reality Maitreya means the number four Buddha.

Whatever is or should be, should be now—that one who should give the entire science for the next 2,500 years, as it was in the case of Gautama. From the time of Gautama up to now there has been no news, nothing really new.

Arica is new. We have built over Gautama and gone further.

As far as I can see we are the only ones at present. Now this is the key: in reality Maitreya is not number five but number four, which is absolutely clear, because Maitreya is the bodhisattva of *Amoghasiddhi.* So we can say that the first Buddha was the bodhisattva for *Aksobhya*—for the realization of the light. The second was the bodhisattva of *Ratnasambhava*—for the realization of equality. The third is the realization of *Amitabha*—that makes the middle way, Gautama completely. The fourth comes from Amoghasiddhi, which means the 'will of realization', so that has to mean the science of how to do it. The final one is unity. In an internal analysis we find that. This is completely accurate, though, if you see, it's just showing the process of humanity as one.

Q: Who are you?

OSCAR: It's not up to me to say that. Reality will say that. Now I'm not going to say it; no one is going to say it, but reality will if it is so. Look, in this sense I would hate to be cheating myself. That's why perhaps I always prefer up to this point to take my chances, because it's a proof. If we are going to fail, fantastic, the sooner the better, because it is more economical like that. In another way, if we are not going to fail and that's how it is, beautiful, then we can really have precision and timing.

Q: What does it mean to fail or not to fail?

OSCAR: Suppose that Arica doesn't do it or is not the method. Up to the point that I know it is, I don't know of anything better; I know there is no better way to my knowledge. So that's where I am. But it doesn't give me anything extra to know you are so and so and that is such and such. On the contrary, if I were to go to that kind of thinking, it would be very much against my way of being, because, you know, I go a different way. Somehow the warrior attitude has gone so very deeply within me that I don't forget the lessons. I know perfectly well what true humility is; on that point I am not a bluffer. I know that by experience and because it is wiser to be like that.

I know anyhow that this game is a war. I know that all this has been a war, a war of the spirit. Well, that is understood, but a war was needed for knowing how to act with the necessary caution, for really knowing how to move.

Q: What is the realization taking place now?

OSCAR: The method for realization, the method of how to become complete. I say that the Arica method does it; I say I don't know any better.

Q: Are we seeing the birth of this method in the culture right now?

OSCAR: Yes, exactly right.

The thing is this. In Arica while we were growing up, the indications were passed as you pass indications to an expert, to a real expert, a real scientist, in the most sophisticated work in a laboratory. When the talk is between extremely sophisticated men, the simplicity with which they talk is amazing. It is the most anti-scientific thing; they communicate internally, and each knows with precision what the other one is saying, more than with the most scientific language, because they are speaking between experts. They can transmit things accurately, even though they say it to one another sloppily. One does a drawing and one looks and the other understands instantaneously; he doesn't need more.

Okay. I wanted that all the time in Arica, mostly at the beginning, and later on because it maintained a level, a very high standard. You know, in Arica the reality has made us have a different kind of language, but somehow I have put impulse in it because I knew how important it is afterwards to have a technical kind of communication with richness that doesn't lose the quality of the live experience and that doesn't become completely stuck, but mostly also because it makes a group that speaks differently.

This makes the seed of the experience. Then, you see, this training at times forces them almost to interpret and discuss it, and all that has made the muscle and has made the brotherhood, of course, in the most beautiful sense of the word in Arica. We are not going to talk so much to technicians, so to speak, because we are going more to the general public. Now we need to be extraordinarily accurate.

So if you see, for those indications I just say exactly what to do, but I don't do them myself in the sense of saying, "Now you raise the left arm and you do that and that," because I forget all those details. Myself, I don't do it. I go quickly to where I really have a problem and then I start working there. So for these kinds of instructions I need other people writing them in detail to see if they can be understood, and then checking with me until we have the instructions perfectly clear. I have to guarantee that there are other people who understand it. Now we are doing that. But that also means that we say these are our final instructions, something that was not possible for me to give before. It would just have gone out in the worst way.

Q: What is the meaning of 'It is now'?

OSCAR: The meaning of 'It is now' is that now we are going to become the universal culture for the first time. We never had a universal culture; we had a pseudo-universal culture. Mathematics here or in Moscow or London are the same; it's more or less a universal tongue, but it is not completely universal because it doesn't allow understanding between human beings.

That is to say, our science is not complete. You know Alexis Carrel? Fifty years ago or so, I guess, he wrote a book where he points out something very obvious: we have different sciences, he says, but we don't have the science of human being. In reality that was his argument: we don't have the science of human being, and we are very far from having it. He tried in that book to give some possible points for that, but not one has any value at all. Now, of course, I say that we *do* have the science of human being.

OBSERVATIONS ON ARICA

Interview by Antonio Huneeus, 1976

CHILEAN JOURNALIST Antonio Huneeus published a two-part interview with Oscar, translated from Spanish, in *The Pears of Aphrodite,* a mimeographed newsletter to the Washington, D.C. Arica family. Likening what had so far been published about Arica to "the tip of an iceberg," Huneeus attempted to probe a little deeper, seeking further explanations of trialectic reasoning and scientific mysticism.

Huneeus inquired about the science of the yantras used by Arica, some of which were then on display in New York City and Santiago, Chile. Arica's yantras are graphic designs that follow laws of form and color, and transmit precise energies to our inner being. Each yantra used in Arica meditations is designed for a specific purpose. It is interesting to note Oscar's responses to questions about the Arica theory, which sometimes, as in this interview, provide basic explanations that shed light on the thought processes leading to a rational and logical understanding of the unity.

On the subject of the metasociety, Oscar said, "What you should stress in your article is that between us there is unity.... In the metasociety people know the instrument that is the psyche so well that they read each other completely."

Antonio Huneeus. "*Pears* interviews Oscar." *Pears of Aphrodite.* January 22, 1976. "*Pears* interviews Oscar. Part II." *Pears of Aphrodite.* April 8, 1976.

ANTONIO HUNEEUS: First I would like to know the relationship between the method and the name of the city of Arica. Why did you take that name, and why was it attractive to begin there?

OSCAR ICHAZO: Well, as far back as 1960, I had started considering the idea of forming a small school. More than a small school, I thought of a small group that could work together and develop the method that I had finally been able to put together in a systematic way. First we met in Santiago, and later we started the first group in Arica. In 1968 I told some friends from Santiago that I was leaving for Arica. Why we chose Arica is obvious. It is an extremely attractive city—modern, with easy access and communication to the outside and at the same time, an isolated city. So it offers both the possibility for fast contact and the possibility of real isolation. Also, the uniformity of its climate allowed us to do long exercises and certain types of work with endurance and perseverance without having to oppose the climate and the environment. The climate of Arica is not only mild, it is incredible. Usually in places where the climate is mild there is an excess of mosquitoes and things of that nature. This does not happen in Arica. The natural environment is exceptional. The native Arican is peaceful, tranquil, imaginative and happy, and the city itself is happy and has a lightness difficult to find elsewhere. Because of that lightness and good humor, you can lead a relatively private life, as private a life as you want. Arica gives you that freedom.

Q: How did the change from Arica to New York come about?

OSCAR: This was not a spontaneous occurrence; there was certain movement leading to it. Once the ten-month training in Arica was completed, I made the decision to continue the work in New York. The group unanimously thought we should go to the West Coast and not to the East Coast. I simply said we were going to New York and, of course, I gave my basic reasons. If it were possible to do any serious work, it had to be done in a place where it would have major repercussions. I understood precisely all the difficulties that working in New York would bring. The first thing the group told me was that New York is one of the most difficult cities in the United States. And as far as mysticism goes, it was precisely the city in which we could expect to find the least amount of help. New York was viewed as the antithesis of mystical work. Here the economic movement, materialism, tends to occupy first place. Nevertheless, New York has a spectacular condition for change. New York is a city that is incredibly spiritualized and human. I have seen New York change radically in the five years I have been here.

Once we moved here, it was my idea to call the movement Arica. The group readily accepted this name; undoubtedly we all felt deep gratitude to the city which had respected our studies and allowed us to work in complete freedom. The kindness of the people of Arica toward the group as a whole, and the fact that our movement had begun in Arica made this the natural thing to do. The Americans who had come to work with me in Arica were people of some resonance. Almost all of them are still in the School. Even though the group was only fifty people, the repercussions they created were tremendous, and they were already known as the Arica group. Nevertheless, my intention had always been to call the movement Arica.

Q: One of the brochures says Arica, in the Quechua language of the Andean Indians, means 'open door'.

OSCAR: I have no authority to tell you about the exact linguistic validity of that translation. This reference was taken from a brochure published by the Development Commission of the city of Arica. This is where that originated. I never gave it much thought. As I said, I do not exactly know the root of this; nevertheless, it is very beautiful.

Q: I would like to know about the mixture of mysticism and science.

OSCAR: In reality, we do not mix mysticism with science. We do the following. Up to now there has not been a critique of reason, that is, an analysis of reason which really answers the primary question, What is reason? What is that which we call reason? We cannot define reason by its function—that is, by saying reason is that which analyzes. What is analysis? Analysis is to see the elements of a compound thing. Here I am not defining, I am naming the function, but where is the definition?

What is reason? Reason, as we know it, only begins to define two things. Through formal logic it defines identity, that is, reason can define identity. As it is, the identity of something does not take into consideration the fact that reality moves, or what is identical to what in that movement. Then we have a paradox. The result is that logic becomes illogical when faced with reality. Logic does not conform to reality. That is the first aspect of reason.

The other aspect is dialectics, which explains the paradox of change. In dialectics the paradox of change is not irrational. It is rational. It explains itself. Our mind has developed enough to be able to understand the paradox of change. Nevertheless, the paradox of change creates another paradox: the paradox of the infinite. If everything is dialectic, it is a dialectical process; it is a process ad infinitum; it is a causal process. However, we know that the universe is not causal and it is not infinite.

Now, the next step tells us that we must arrive at a new kind of logic, a logic that explains the unity, to find the laws that explain the unity. That is trialectics. I have found them, and they work. From the moment we find this, everything changes totally. All our systems of thought change because we are in another level of thought. Now what happens? If I have the logic by means of which I can demonstrate the unity, then my reason has achieved a level by which it can understand totality. So let's say through reason I have reached mysticism.

Q: Is that what is new?

OSCAR: That is what is new. Before this system, the only way to achieve a religious experience was through faith, which you either have or do not have. If you have faith, there is grace. If you do not have faith, there is no grace. This is obvious; there is no question about it. However, if we can explain the unity to ourselves—not feel it but explain it—then things change fundamentally. We are in another world. From that moment on, everything else is defined from that one point, that perspective.

I start from very basic questions. The first ones that have to be answered are: What is reason? What is consciousness? What is mind? What is the psyche? What are its components? What are all their elements? We also have to answer, What is gravity? I do not believe the fairy tale that attraction exists between the earth and the sun, or that an apple three kilometers away from here has something to do with a string bean that is here. I do not swallow that story. The childishness of the concept is enormous. Newton was not childish. Newton was Newton. He said, let's *suppose* that two bodies attract each other. That 'suppose' has been forgotten by everyone, and that they attract has become dogma.

Q: And this does not happen in reality?

OSCAR: Of course not. The concept that we now have of the universe is totally invalid. It is inconceivable to think that the origin of the galaxies is cosmic waste that unites and reunites, circulates and creates gravity, becomes a spiral which gets larger and larger and finally explodes, and that out of this the suns and planets are born. We cannot continue believing this childishness. Furthermore, the theory we have about biological evolution does not make it. It does not function in reality. Reality totally contradicts the theory of selection of the species. We cannot continue swallowing such a pill.

What the Arica system does, the first thing it does, is to describe the psyche, analyze its origin, precisely identify each one of its points, and trace exact maps of consciousness. To do this we use the method of 'the logic of the unity'. I call it objective thought. Once we know the maps of consciousness, we know exactly what we can expect. We then know what we need to do to produce a definite effect. We can select the paths much better. The parameters are established and the variables are analyzed. It is no more and no less than a real scientific basis for analysis. So we can say that Arica represents the discovery of the logic of the unity and that on that basis we make a complete description of the psyche and of the fundamental problems we need to know about.

As long as we continue thinking that attraction exists between the planets, we are in the same position as people were before the discovery of America, when they believed the world was flat. So long as someone still has the idea that the earth is flat, his psyche has not sufficiently evolved. We are in a very similar position. Obviously, the potency of our psyche changes with certain information.

Q: What is the need for a metasociety?

OSCAR: Everybody has talked about it and it has been proven that man is in danger of extinction. I have nothing else to add to what has already been said about this. It has been repeated many times. What are even closer to our times are the economic problems that have been encountered. They are of such tremendous magnitude and so difficult that it is hard to envision how the world can go through this violent crisis. If we do not start moving the machinery backwards, extinction is simply going to come from all sides—pollution, overpopulation, etc. This matter is very serious. We are so near the precipice, so close to chaos, that we simply must stop and meditate.

But now the central idea of this theory is that if we have a scientific method of developing man, and if it is possible to develop his total possibilities, then not only is a new man produced, but obviously what man is a product of and what he produces, his society, also changes radically. I call it the metasociety to show that it is really beyond what we know now. Metasociety for us is a point in which there are no longer relations, but there is unity, between the people who compose that society. Because a society of relations is a society of fighting; it's a society of battle and of contradictions, and necessarily so, because that is its level.

In the metasociety we speak of unity for the simple reason that all the people of that society would know the instrument that is the psyche so well that they would read each other completely. This is not strange. This already exists inside Arica. Between us there is no relation, there is unity, and if that unity doesn't exist, then the defense mechanisms of that organism, the body of Arica, are instantaneously produced. Reductions are produced. If somebody is not in unity with another, the other person reduces him, reduces his ego, as we call it, his personal position. Now the personal position is not good or bad, but it is a level, and inside Arica we do not want that level.

Q: Is it more direct?

OSCAR: It is direct and it cannot be any different. That is the definition we give to Arica.

Q: A society in unity?

OSCAR: A society in unity.

Q: And is that the only way to go through the crisis?

OSCAR: Yes. The only way. It is very simple: if a unified society emerges, we have a society a hundred times stronger, a hundred times more intelligent, a hundred times more capable, a hundred times more daring, a hundred times more creative, a hundred times more everything, with a multiplying effect that is almost unbelievable. It can be done. If these societies become a metasociety, we jump, because their level of realization would be different.

Q: About three years ago we were told that humanity had only ten years to solve its problems. So can we expect seven years now?

OSCAR: Yes. No more. But what we say is this: This is the time that we have to become aware of the danger of our present situation. Of course that is going to happen. Not only that, but we must become aware that we have to change, and start changing. There has to be enough time to know that human beings can achieve a higher degree of consciousness.

Here we must say that what has taken a lot of work was forming the body of Arica. It has taken time to do each successive training until we reached the necessary level, which is what we call the 'Cutting of the Diamond'. We did the 'Cutting of the Diamond' after five years of consecutive work. This is a tremendous speed when you consider that it includes the realization of all the intermediate steps. In order to elaborate a rational system that produces inner development from beginning to end, it is necessary to go through many steps, or it is not produced. That is definite. Now in Arica we know exactly what has to be done. Everything has been measured and proven completely, not in one person, but in hundreds of persons. That is the value that Arica now has to the world. We will have more success, too, because we have a well-proven method, a well-tested method; each one of the exercises, each one of the parts that compose the system, has been tested and proven. But first we had to form a body, truly a body. Now that has been achieved; we are already in the metasociety.

One cannot theorize about the metasociety. It must be lived, and when you are in it, you can transmit it. Aricans know this. When Aricans go anywhere, they become like catalyzers; there is a transmission of a message that is completely alive, which the person carries inside himself and which is manifested in the way he walks, the way he looks, the general expression of his being vibrating in a certain way. In some way his vibrations are of trust; he vibrates security, tranquillity, happiness—not exactly like the tinkling of a little bell, but happiness nonetheless—all the things our psyche always wishes for. So a person who is with an Arican starts to wish very quickly to have the same things himself, because all of them are desirable. Another thing that happens within a well-developed psyche is that the amount of wants diminishes to an infinitesimal level. The more trivial things lose their importance. You have been in the houses of Aricans; they are really very simple; there are no unnecessary objects. There is a lot of space, and the beauty, the beauty! But at the same time all this is demonstrating a certain type of psyche, a psyche that has eliminated a lot of unnecessary things.

We can say this: once the method has been realized with the right persistence and following the steps that have been measured, the result is so obvious it really doesn't deserve any discussion. Now, up to the present we haven't yet gone to the public; we are going only now. We have received a lot of publicity from the most important press in the U.S. and some parts of Europe, even though I have never really made any motion to attract the press, absolutely none. I have worked with a lot of reserve, with very good reason, naturally, not because I have any dislike of the press—on the contrary, it is very good. But my reason was very simple: I thought it was not yet the moment, because when one is building, one cannot explain his construction. Now our position is different; Arica is finished.

Another thing is that after an effort so constant and so systematized, and conducted really with an iron hand—because that's the way we have worked in Arica, with fear of nothing—we have the result. The result is that we have a school that is incredibly professional in the use of this theory. We have created a profession that—forgive me if I qualify this—is truly of the first strength.

So we have a professional team, really enormously professional. It is not easy to train hundreds of professionals at the same time. What I want to say here is that once the group starts its activity—and that must be now—it should produce a very big result. And the other thing is that the system, the method, the exercises have all been so carefully and so professionally done that they are ready to go out. In fact, they are already in print. And truly speaking, it's a very big thing, a really extensive thing.

Q: What would you like to say about the 'daily routine' and its importance for Arica at this moment?

OSCAR: When you want to do something professionally, you do a routine, and you repeat and repeat and repeat it until it is really so loose that you don't have to think about what you are doing any more. Then, once you don't have to think about it, you are really doing it seriously, sharply, naturally. It is the same as when you play the piano. First you have the routine; you practice until it gets into your hands. When it is in your hands, then you can interpret it; then you can put in emotions and all that, but not before.

Q: Recently in Santiago there was a public exhibition of the yantras. I would like you to talk about the yantras. What is their tradition? How does Arica use them? And can they be considered decorative, a future art?

OSCAR: The origin of the yantras is inner vision that can be contemplated in a certain state. The patterns exist inside our being in depth, so they can't be taken as pure invention. Now, inside those existing patterns I have used the systems of symbology of form and symbology of color that are very old and come from the tradition of the White Brotherhood, as it is called in the Orient. Exactly what the White Brotherhood is would be too difficult to explain right now, but let's say that the principles are those of the White Brotherhood. Now, these same principles have been considerably elaborated. I have used a formula and this has taken me to another type of definition. But here we must understand definitions of a mathematical type in terms of the result of form in relation to the criterion of space and the criterion of time. But that's another thing. The yantras are the result of all that process, because what I found is that those patterns which exist in our being are very precise. Maybe that is the strength of the yantras. They are so direct that one starts to work with a yantra and—you must have had the experience—the experience comes almost immediately, so it is without any doubt that something very measured and very scientific exists, since it works all the time.

Q: It is like they put the psyche in order.

OSCAR: Exactly. They are for that. They are existing patterns of the psyche that, when we see them, remind us only of what is already there. This can be violent. It produces a remembering of what is there, or awakens it, we could say. Without any doubt it is one of the most powerful methods that exist. Sincerely, I don't know of any other thing that produces a true experience in the space of seconds. Concentrate on one of the yantras, open it well, and you have the experience of, as you say, the psyche becoming ordered in a very determined way.

Now, about the science of yantras itself. We accept that nine levels of the work exist, so the first work with the yantras is the simplest. Then in other levels the meditation becomes very complex. What do we want to come to? We want to come to this: There comes a time when, on the basis of the eighty-one existing yantras, we have an extensive ideogram, an extensive ideogrammatic system, let's say, with which we can make psychic elaborations that are impossible in any other way. Because once one learns to think in 'yantras', so to speak, one's thoughts are different. Now, of course, all this is only with the objective of producing a psychic widening to the limit of its possibilities.

Q: What is the exact time and place of your birth?

OSCAR: I was born in Roboré, Santa Cruz, Bolivia at seven o'clock in the morning on the twenty-fourth of July, 1931. Roboré is a very little town between Santa Cruz and Corumba in Brazil.

Q: Did your family own some land in that region?

OSCAR: No. My father is military by profession and he was serving on the frontier. That is the duty of the military. He was in charge of a little frontier command there, and that is the place where I was born. At that time, Roboré was really a very little village.

Q: I am very interested in knowing some facts about your life.

OSCAR: Well, I've had a very complex life. Anyhow, I have found that my difficulty in trying to explain my life is that it has been so complex. I can see, at the same time, I've had some main lines, so to speak. This isn't so strange; everything in man has that. At the same time that he is in mysticism, he is in sentiments, and then, you know, the human being is a very complex thing. But it depends on what you want to know.

Q: I would like to know something about your trip to Afghanistan.

OSCAR: Well, I don't know what to say. The first time I went to the Orient was in 1956.

Q: Was that after you lived in that house in Buenos Aires?

OSCAR: Yes. Now, the part in Buenos Aires is very simple. There was a group of people and not one of them was Latin American. For some reason they chose Buenos Aires. They chose it because it was comfortable. At least one of them in the group was really a millionaire, and all the rest were more or less well-provided for. It wasn't formal. Somehow the millionaire in the group was trying to implement his idea that it was possible to synthesize all mysticism, that it was the time to do it and to present it. He was a very high mystic and all his friends there were of the very first class. Now, although the idea was to make the group in Buenos Aires, it never happened because, number one, they were never all together, because they were too busy, or surrounded by disciples at the same time, and also it was difficult for them to leave their places to come to Buenos Aires. So in reality most of the time was spent in communicating—this one is going and the other is coming.

Q: So there was a lot of circulation.

OSCAR: A lot of circulation with very little result as effort in the work itself. They didn't do much about the work, but they talked about things until eventually they started really working with me. It was somehow quite sloppy in the sense that one would teach me one thing and the other another thing. It was very eclectic because they were trying to see different things. There was never a complete line. Even though there was a point at which it almost came, it never really happened. That's what I can say about it.

Q: From there did you get recommendations to different places in the Orient?

OSCAR: Oh, yes! You know, they were extraordinarily important for me; they opened doors for me to the most secret places, places that were very difficult to get into, almost impossible.

Q: Are all these places still functioning?

OSCAR: No. They used to be in the Pamir but now the Pamir is a controlled place because it is a strategic point. So it is no longer a mystical point; now it is used for missiles. The Pamir used to be such a far-out place, because there was nothing. It is a plateau with almost nothing, and because of that condition it was possible to have these kinds of places. They were called monasteries, because that's what they looked like, but in reality they were little villages of, at most, three or four houses together.

Q: Were they of the Sufi tradition?

OSCAR: They are more than the Sufi tradition. We've got to understand here all the Muslim world—what it is, what has produced it.

Q: And now have they moved?

OSCAR: Yes. The center is now in Kabul. There is another big center in Qandahar, another big center in Herat; Mashhad also, not so big but important, and in Karbala. Those are the most important places where these people are. And you know, the thing is that once one door is opened, it is well-opened, because it is not just a matter of opening. It is that they accept your qualities for what they are. They are so demanding, so strict, so tough, if you want. But once they open the door, so to speak, they really do.

A SCIENTIFIC APPROACH

Interview by Rick Fields, 1976

BORN IN BOLIVIA in 1931, Oscar Ichazo trained in the martial arts while still a boy, and experienced psychotropic drugs and shamanism through contact with the Indians of the Andes. He was instructed in Zen, Sufism, the Kaballah, and Gurdjieffian cosmology by masters in Latin America. He then traveled widely in the East to do advanced work in martial arts, learn the higher yogas, and study Buddhism, Confucianism, alchemy, and the *I Ching*. This list leaves out his extensive study of science and physiology—he was, for example, assisting in the dissection of cadavers at a La Paz medical school at the age of twelve—and the wide range of his readings in philosophy and literature.

The following is an excerpt of a two-hour interview with Oscar at Arica headquarters. The style of Oscar's English is strongly colored by his native Spanish, which lends a unique flavor to his conversation.

RICK FIELDS: How can one man have had the time to thoroughly study all of the spiritual disciplines you have without just getting impressions and tastes? Do you feel you have thoroughly digested all this material?

Rick Fields. "A talk with Oscar Ichazo." *New Age Journal*. June, 1976.

OSCAR ICHAZO: Oh, yes. I will tell you why. Because, without wanting it, I got trained to a very fast and scientific way of seeing things and just taking the bones out of them. That was how I have studied all my life. It is like learning languages. The first is very difficult to learn. The second one is easier. If you know four, any language is easy. Once you have eight, it's like you jump. In Arica study we say that you jump the MMP (the material manifestation point). It's so easy.

Another thing was that from the very beginning in the Orient I was recognized as a man who has achieved what's called the satori condition. So from the beginning, I was respected differently. I was not treated as a disciple—never—not even by those who were very high in the realization.

Also, I was going with some very fine presentations from common friends. I would be presented as a friend, not as a disciple. Details, but, you know, these are details that count enormously.

Also, if I went inside any training or anything, I would know a lot about it before, so I was never a beginner in anything. I was already somebody who did it.

Well, so from that finally comes the method.

The method is dividing the consciousness into all that it is, seeing all that you can do, and seeing exactly the line of purification of consciousness that is enlightenment. For the first time it can be done without faith, with total security that if you do the method it is going to work.

Q: Isn't that a big promise?

OSCAR: It is, but we can make the promise after we have the experience with at least five thousand people, and they always succeed.

Q: Do you mean that everybody who's done the Arica training is enlightened?

OSCAR: Depending on what level. Say about the 'Diamond' level, they certainly are.

Q: What is this I hear about levels? If you're working on yourself and you're looking at what's going on directly, that seems to me to be very important, rather than waking up in the morning and feeling, "I'm on this level or I'm on that level."

OSCAR: When it is accurate, there is no doubt where you are, and that is very beautiful to know. What is beautiful in the Arica system is that you always have that measure; you know where you are.

Q: In what sense are the levels scientific? Is it a hard science?

OSCAR: No. And in a way it is absolutely accurate. We have a scientific approach to an organism. If you know how the heart works you have the science of the heart, and you can count the beats and you know what resistance it has.

Now, in the same way we have the measurement of the psyche. We know how much resistance it has, how many environments or domains it has, how many thoughts it can have, and no more. We know when and what psychosis is, what it causes, how it works. It's a total scientific approach.

Another reason we say it is scientific is because we go with the approach of experience. We are experiential. We don't say to somebody, get faith because with that you are going to be cured. We say, do this accurately and you are going to have a result.

Q: Well, something like *est* seems to work the same way.

OSCAR: No. The experience that they get in *est* is really, as much as I've read, as much as is published, absolutely false.

Q: And yet people who take it feel totally convinced by it.

OSCAR: Of course you can have that kind of suggestion, if you want. And the suggestion can be rather strong if it's validated with certain types of reasoning.

For example, Castaneda, at the end of his books, speaks about stopping the world, something nobody can do, not Castaneda, not his imagined character Don Juan; nobody can stop the world. But you can really stop your mind. But you know, that is the trick of Castaneda—trying to say nothing new about something very old. And he makes nonsense.

Q: You don't think Castaneda or Don Juan has a genuine teaching?

OSCAR: Absolutely not.

Q: Do you think he made it up?

OSCAR: Absolutely. Number one, you know there do not exist people who fly as he said. That is good for Spiderman. Number two, the sorcery that he says is Indian is not Indian at all. He doesn't understand Indians. I come from Indian country. He comes from Peru, but he's from the coast. He's from a Spanish culture that denies Indian culture, despises Indian culture and doesn't understand it at all. Well, so he's coming from a point where they don't have that understanding. I am from a point where that understanding is complete, because my country is an Indian country.

The sorcery in Don Juan is Western sorcery. That is witchcraft as we know it. So it comes from witchcraft; Indians don't know that kind of thing. The idea of a warrior is not an Indian idea. It is a Chinese idea, because if there were a warrior thing in the Indian culture, there would be a martial art and there is none. The final thing is the Diamond Sutra involved in this thing. Instead of saying stop your mind, he says stop the world. One thing with concepts, and mostly with mystical concepts, is that they don't allow you to manipulate them at random.

Another thing, *est* says you create your own universe. That's nonsense.

Q: Well, they say you create your experience.

OSCAR: No, you create your world, is what they say. Now, that idea is absolutely true in the sense that your consciousness does, but you don't manipulate your consciousness because you are not yet the owner of that consciousness. If you were the owner of that consciousness, you could do that.

Q: Well, that's what they claim to give people, the ownership of their consciousness.

OSCAR: You know, Erhard is really just working with slogans. That, of course, comes across very well to an audience that is going to get his suggestion very strongly for a certain period of time, and after that they are going to just break their necks, and they are going to see that in reality the world is not like that at all.

Q: Doesn't Arica use suggestion, for example, as in the repetitions?

OSCAR: Now, you know, the repetitions would be rather dangerous if they weren't something that belongs to the purity of consciousness, and consciousness cannot deny that. For example, "We are One. We are One." Whether we accept it or not, it's a fact. "I am Consciousness." We don't deny that, you know. So each repetition is a repetition that is not going to produce an effect of suggestion in you, but rather an effect of enlightenment and reassurance of something that is basically true.

Q: Does Arica have a sense of humor?

OSCAR: Oh, yes—Arica has a lot.

Q: About itself, about its own work?

OSCAR: Naturally. We are all laughing about ourselves. This is something that is established in Arica. They imitate me or imitate the training, trainers, and the trainees, and what we do. And what in Arica is very deep is the sense of equality that we have. Nevertheless, we accept the levels, and in Arica everybody accepts that the superior level is certainly a superior level. Because for us it would be the same equality like it is in the normal society. You have a baby that is a human being, as you are a human being. In that sense, that baby and you have the same validity. He is an equal. But he doesn't know what you know or what I know. And in that sense he's not equal. In Arica, we are all equal in the sense that we're Aricans, but there are some who know more than others.

Q: Where do you fit in?

OSCAR: I did the entire path. I know the entire path, really. Otherwise I wouldn't be teaching about it. I have achieved all the conditions. I know what it is exactly.

Q: I notice from your book that the method works without a teacher for the first seven steps, but then at the last two some direct transmission is necessary.

OSCAR: That I do say.

Q: So aren't you saying that a guru is necessary on that level?

OSCAR: On that level, again, it wouldn't be a position of a guru, but you need a communion with a leader completely, without being in the position of guru.

Q: What is the difference between that and the guru?

OSCAR: The difference is that the guru is energizing you constantly. That is his blessing; that is why he's a guru. So let's say, a guru is like a radiant being that has enormous mystical strength, like a fountain that is permanently providing the disciples with that pure strength. In the work of Arica, even in the last part, there is not that. There is no direct input of me over the students. Nevertheless, in certain situations I might need to do that, and I wouldn't deny it if I feel I have to, but that's not the ideal. The ideal is for that not to happen.

Q: Are you enlightened?

OSCAR: Absolutely, beyond any question or doubt. I don't have any questions about it. And if I did have a little question about it, I wouldn't be teaching.

MAKING A MYSTICAL SCHOOL

Interview by Susan Lydon, 1978

THE NO TIME TIMES, a tabloid newspaper that appeared monthly for most of 1977 and 1978, was born during a period of commercial activity in which the proliferation of Arica-related businesses needed a central place from which to advertise goods and services to the community at large.

Artistically, the paper's intentions were to explore the journalistic possibilities offered by the unique and comprehensive intellectual framework which a study of the Arica theory can provide. To this end *No Time Times* writers reviewed movies, books, and cultural events from the perspective of trialectics and protoanalysis, covered local visits by spiritual dignitaries, and commented on subjects like the martial arts.

In its interviews with Oscar Ichazo, the paper attempted to illuminate the concepts and theory of Arica for readers encountering them for the first time. The focus of the interviews was on providing basic definitions of terms and finding a workable answer to the deceptively simple question, What is Arica?

Susan Lydon. "Making a mystical school: NTT interviews Oscar Ichazo on the first eight years." *No Time Times*. July-August, 1978.

Susan Lydon. "NTT interview with Oscar Ichazo. Part II: The Mission of Arica." *No Time Times*. March-April, 1979.

SUSAN LYDON: You've said lots of times that you're not a guru. What's the difference between you and a guru?

OSCAR ICHAZO: Well, I would say it like this. A guru is a self-realized man in totality who becomes an example for his students to follow. The difference between that and the approach of Arica is that it doesn't need one example to follow; it wants to understand everybody in his own process without the necessity for personal guidance. At the same time, I am in the position of a guide, in the sense of guiding the School as a whole. I don't do personal work with people. I always would work with a group of Aricans, precisely to jump beyond the step of personal guidance, and I just keep the situation of a guide for the School as a whole. I am not a personal guide. Also, I don't show myself as an example. I have said to the School many, many times that I am not an example of anything. We are trying to understand ourselves scientifically. And why do we say scientifically? Because then the method can be passed systematically without the intervention of personal input that would be the natural way of a guru.

Q: Many people notice that in Arica there are no strict rules about eating and drinking and sex.

OSCAR: No, not at all. Our sense of not having rules is that if you are dealing with the entire range of consciousness, you don't need rules because you know what you are doing. So you would live within your own limits. You would know those limits and their parameters. What we really ask is that Aricans take complete responsibility for themselves and be willing to take care of themselves the best possible way. And for that we are giving a theory, we are giving a method, and we are giving a means to follow it that works.

Q: Basically, how would you explain what Arica is?

OSCAR: Well, Arica provides a new theory about the psyche; it provides a new method of scientific comprehension. And because Arica has this theory about the psyche, it has also evolved a method for making the psyche fulfilled and clear in the sense of being able to develop its potential to its fullest, if that is possible. That's the aim of Arica—by having the complete and entire knowledge of our psyche, to enable ourselves to handle our problems better, faster, easier and clearer.

Q: What is new in the Arica system?

OSCAR: What Arica is proposing in this theory is, number one, to make a fundamental revision of the entire knowledge about the human psyche. That's one thing. Another thing is that for the first time, we know the entire structure of the psyche. That is, for the first time we know all the possible logics that the human brain can think. I am saying another thing. Until now, Western philosophy couldn't go beyond Immanuel Kant's criticism of reason. Arica is proposing a complete advance with trialectics. And with that goes an entire critique of reason. So what we propose is entirely new. I mean in the entire sense. We are proposing a complete transformation. A final transformation.

Q: You are saying that these are the limits of human knowledge?

OSCAR: Well, the limits of human knowledge also involve the understanding of what kind of universe we live in, something that at this very moment we don't know.

Q: What sort of impact do you expect these ideas to have on the world?

OSCAR: These new ideas have enormous impact in the sense that they are going to change the human psyche. It's the same as in the time when the idea that the earth is not the center of the universe was not only unacceptable, it was shocking. Or the idea that the earth is round was totally unacceptable. It was seen as flat; how could it be round? But there is a moment when it is just proven. And when it's proven, all the arguments against it become absolutely meaningless. There the human consciousness changes. Can you see the change of that time? In the moment that it was proven that we are not the center of the universe, we are just one more planet around the sun, and we are not even one of the bigger ones, the human psyche changed.

Q: Well, it's very shocking to think that the human psyche

has limits, and that they can be known and measured. How does Arica go about proving those things?

OSCAR: What we are doing is specifically in two areas: in the area of self-realization and in the area of clarification of consciousness. But we don't go in the area of religion. Religion means faith and has truths that have already been said by true prophets and true avatars all around the world. So in religion there is no news. But in the field of self-realization, there is always some room for improvement for the simple reason that our culture, inasmuch as it evolves, presents new issues for our consciousness to deal with. It is natural in the history of humanity that every time and every epoch has to have its own ways of realization. Now, that is what our technological society needs to work on more. Arica is trying in that sense to fit with our time and with the natural process of evolution of human history, to match the problems that evolving society presents.

Q: What's the difference between self-realization and clarification of consciousness?

OSCAR: Self-realization is the moment that you want to improve yourself. In self-realization could be sports, could be any kind of training that improves you; meditation of course is here, all types of meditation; spiritual exercises are here, all types of spiritual exercises. But after you do them there is another field beyond that, that is, to clarify your consciousness to the point that you recognize reality as it is. Now, when reality is recognized as it is, it is then very easy to go to the next step, and that is the final step of human consciousness, that is, the field of faith. But we don't talk about that, it's already been said.

Q: Where do you see Arica in relation to the evolution of humanity?

OSCAR: As we know, now humanity is facing perhaps the most difficult period of all its history, since we really have very dramatic demands to meet, and because of that, we need a method that can match the speed of the problems. It has to be very fast, because we don't have much time left, and it has to make the solution to these problems easier. We don't say that Arica has the solution to these problems, not at all. But we say that a very clear understanding of the human psyche would indeed be a very good asset to have. It is not only important; it is fundamental. And that is what Arica is all about.

Q: Is that why you started Arica?

OSCAR: I was working just for myself, but always believing that if I were to find some news I would write about it. The need for a school never came to my mind until the moment that the material was completed and it was obvious that such a thing could not be handled just by one man. For that we needed a school, that is, a larger consciousness, for the simple reason that a larger number of human consciousnesses is the only possible and reasonable way to present this. So it started in the moment that I was completely convinced that it was necessary to do it. I started eleven years ago, and it took me about two years until I had a place and I could really start saying, "I have some news and we can work differently with complete responsibility about it." The School started with the first group that went to Chile. That training started on July 1, 1970, and that is the sentimental birthday. But the real birth of the School was in New York, on the thirty-first of December, 1971.

Q: And how did you know then that the School was a reality?

OSCAR: Because the first group could pass the same information to the second group even though we were working pretty differently in both trainings. The spirit of the School was then mature, and I knew that we were going to be together for the entire process and the entire work. It came to me very clear that it was like that, and it was very sharp.

The moment that we made that simple ceremony, the School started. It was obvious that we were going to continue, that it was important to do this work. We had already faced all the difficulties of doing this work in New York, in a first class hotel, and we had put in all the worst hurdles to jump, and it happened that everybody did. Both groups jumped at that point. Then it was a true fact that there was a school, a true fact that there were roots that were alive.

Q: What in Arica has been incorporated from traditional methods?

OSCAR: Because Arica is a different approach, it is going to have different methods. We can't say that we are the first method of meditation. Meditation is as old as humanity. So we are one more method; we are not saying we are *the* method. But yes, we are saying that we have a different approach. We are approaching it by a different parameter. Because if you have not scientifically described what the psyche is, then you don't know with what you are working. Then it becomes a very big work to do. It takes a long time. But if you have all the parameters of the psyche, you can deal with it easier, faster, more comprehensibly, and in the way that our psyche has been structured by our own society. We live in a technological society, a scientific society. So if you present a scientific method, it is more easily grasped. The Arica type of meditation is totally new. Of course, there are certain specific parameters in meditation that are always going to be the same in any type of meditation you do. So in that sense we start as it traditionally has been started. Arica has the same goal. But there are things like the *Kinerhythm* exercise—that is not a new exercise, but has been synthesized by me in a new form that doesn't contradict the tradition and makes the experience more available to our time.

Q: Where does the exercise come from?

OSCAR: This kind of exercise has really been developed in the Pamir a long time ago. It is well known that most of the meditations come from the Pamir.

Q: What's the Pamir?

OSCAR: The Pamir is a high plateau that has always been looked to as the traditional point from where different forms of meditation come. Padmasambhava, who founded the theory of the tradition of Tibetan Buddhism, came from the Pamir in the sense that he first studied there. Because the Pamir was a point of encounter of cultures, it was the place where methods of all the knowledge of these cultures were synthesized. It was the meeting place of the Chinese culture, of the Tartar culture, and the Arabic culture, and the Hindu culture. So it has been always a kind of university where these different cultures would be studied. And from that evolved the new material and new plans. There was a method of kinesthetic movement for deep concentration, and from that I developed the kinesthetic movements by compressing them to a high degree. This has two advantages. In one way it is easier to do in a limited space; we don't need the big spaces for kinesthetic movements which have always been required. Also, they required a pretty good silence and certain practices of a strong *pranayama*. Now all that has been synthesized in one, in what we know now as *Kinerhythm*. So they are traditional techniques that have been synthesized, compressed, and at the same time made easier. I would say that they are deeper. There is less to do, and it takes less time and less space, but it is more intense. Our psyche also is accustomed to that intensity because we are dealing with a technological society that moves intensely. So it is natural for us to accept that intensity.

Q: It seems that the way Arica trainings work is through lots of exercises, and different ones work for different people.

OSCAR: What the trainings are trying to do is fulfill all the parameters of the psyche, physically, emotionally, intellectually, and spiritually. The Arica training is dramatically successful because it is worked in all these four parameters at one time. And it is worked intensely. Now, suppose you are in a training and your physical parameter is better than your spiritual parameter. That changes with the training and at the end of the training you have a very uniform result. I am not saying that in the training everybody is following the same pace; it moves in accord of personal process. For some, this is more intense or that is more intense; there are always differences. The trainings have been designed to deal with these basic difficulties at the beginning, but inasmuch as the training goes inside, it becomes more demanding and more unifying, and at the end it is really very amazing to see that the results are the same for everybody.

Q: Is that partly from the group through the law of communicating vessels?

OSCAR: Absolutely. It is one of the things that we employ. It has to be group work because we know group work means concentration of time and with that comes acceleration of process.

Q: Is Arica the first to go with group work in that way in the trainings?

OSCAR: With this intensity, yes. I have never seen this kind of work in that amount that makes a group so tightly knit. We are not the first to work in groups, but the groups that we have are more tied and obviously speed up the entire process.

Q: What in your historical background prepared you for this?

OSCAR: Well, it has taken my entire life. I can't say this or that. I didn't know at the beginning how it was going to end. It was just impossible to say—how could I? At the time it was not my purpose ever to end up founding a school. I never imagined it. I was just working for myself, in very intense training, and with an immense demand of my psyche to bridge that point. I really studied Western science and was at ease with it. But when it became not enough for me, I started trying to seek new methods in the Oriental wisdom that is known to have answers for these problems. And, well, that put me in one tradition and then in another tradition and then in another tradition until there was a point that, well, I don't say I knew all, but let's say, I knew a big percentage of all the schools and all the ways, and I didn't know some. So, I experienced myself and I started understanding that there were not many differences between one and another, and that it was possible in time to structure something new.

Q: What's been the process of the School, the development of the School so far?

OSCAR: It has been amazingly strong and we have been very sharp with our timing. To build a school takes time. It is inevitable. And we did it in a minimum because it always has taken many, many years of the life of a guide to form a school. So we really did it in minimum time. It makes you more grateful for the process because to maintain such an amount of people concentrated in such a manner has taken the intense effort of all of us. There have been intense sacrifices in the sense of giving your entire life and your entire input to the School while the School was growing up, with all the difficulties that that means.

Q: How do you feel that the School is going now?

OSCAR: I guess the School has really already achieved an intense maturity. It is understanding its responsibility more clearly because we are all doing the work with the same responsibility and understanding that everybody is doing the job that has to be done. We are very close to the point of saying that the School is ready for dealing with what has to be presented. That is, clear trainings, a more efficient teaching. Now the School has the experience of that. And to build that experience is a difficult thing. To pass the results is easy; the first part is what is difficult. And that's done.

Q: What do you see will happen next?

OSCAR: Now the School is going to take more and more responsibility for this entire movement as it's really happening. There are new associations that work with complete responsiblity for themselves and with complete responsibility also for the theory, the methods, and the general, let's say, principles of the School. The Aricans, with their experience, are the ones that really know what are the best and most efficient ways to teach and to pass the trainings. And eventually the Aricans will have to take the responsibility for the complete management of the Institute and so on.

Q: So if a new student comes to Arica now, all their energy and all their input wouldn't be required.

OSCAR: Not in that way. Not with the intensity that it was.

Q: What do you mean when you speak about the mission, and when will the mission have been completed?

OSCAR: You know, it is a mission in the sense that it is in charge of passing to humanity a new method, a new theory, and new techniques for self-realization and clarification of consciousness that seem to be, from my point of view, the most important issue of our time. So in that sense it is a mission; it is a duty. It is not meant only for a particular group of people. It's for everybody. That's why it is a mission. At the beginning, Arica was founded, and was joined up to this time, by people who were very concerned with these things, and who decided to put their effort, after seeing the results in themselves, toward passing on this theory, method, and techniques. Once you know these things, you immediately remember that it is good for somebody else, so it becomes a normal responsibility.

Q: And when will it have fulfilled its purpose?

OSCAR: It will fulfill its purpose pretty soon, when the entire theory is completely published, when the entire method is completed, when all the courses that Arica offers are completed, and also when the School takes responsibility for itself. You cannot take full responsibility until you have all the tools in your hands, so we have been achieving that goal partially up to this point. We couldn't yet go to a very large public, to very large audiences, although we have seen over 200,000 people pass through different Arica trainings, both large and small. Even though that number is a very big number, it is not a number with which we really influence our society. We are not yet with total strength, with total impact, so to speak. And for that really we still need a little bit more time.

Q: Many journalists and observers view the spiritual movement as being narcissistic. They say people work on themselves for their own personal benefit. What do you think about that?

OSCAR: It is very simple, you know. The better you are, the better you are going to be for everybody. It's a very simple equation. The better you are, the better it is for everybody around you. So to make ourselves better is a duty, because then everything around us just becomes better. Even if it is narcissistic in the beginning, the effects are not. You can say really sharp that it's servitude, but it has to start in us. Then, the better we are, the better is everything around us. But in the next interview we are going to speak more about the spiritual movement.

PART II: THE MISSION OF ARICA

Q: You've said that Arica is a mission. What's a mission?

OSCAR: A mission is a necessity of the entire culture to achieve a higher degree of consciousness. History evolves from one MMP (material manifestation point) to another across missions. When a culture reaches its fulfillment, and a new culture with a new point of view is needed, a mission appears in the planet. A mission is the bridge for changing from one culture to a superior culture. Not to deny the culture that is becoming obsolete, but a mission gives the solutions for making a new culture, since the old one no longer works. A mission is presented in our world in the moment of definitive crisis, when there has to be a change from one culture to a superior one. The bridge is the mission.

In that sense Arica is a mission because it is proposing the solutions for this society to become a higher MMP of society that we call metasociety. Now, that bridge at this point doesn't require news about religion, which, by the way, has already been said. I have insisted on this point. But it requires methods for self-realization and clarification of consciousness, for understanding the parameters of where our culture is, because the answers that we have from the past don't fit our present conditions. And we are not going to have a new culture if these two points are not resolved.

Arica is a mission because it tries to resolve these two points of self-realization and clarification of consciousness. I am not denying that methods for doing this already exist, and that we propose just one more. But this one more is faster. It's the fastest and the most complete that it is possible to present.

Q: Why do we need a really fast method?

OSCAR: Every crisis in the past has had its own parameters and has taken its own time. In our time, because of the speed of our technological society, it is necessary to have a very fast method. It has to be fast because with our media and our communication everything is processed at a high speed. Our material has to have the resistance for moving at a high speed. You construct a plane to break the sound barrier with materials that resist that velocity. In the same way, our culture is moving so fast that we require a method that also resists that speed. That is a very fast one indeed.

Q: What is our movement in society?

OSCAR: Our movement in society is to give society the precise tools for self-realization and clarification of consciousness. We have all those methods. At the same time, these methods will benefit society by creating a style, a new point of view, a new way of behaving, a new way of being in the sense of being in the social domain. I am not here speaking of the transcendental being, but of social behavior. All this creates, to say it in one word, a style, and that style is a wave and that wave is a movement of people that are going toward their realization of the entire society as one solid community. In that sense, it's a movement.

Q: You recently said that until now we have been investing in the School and that the investment is going to return to us by expanding the School.

OSCAR: We are a spiritual movement and investment here has meant investment of energy; we have built a School. We have built, first of all, the people of the School, the teachers. It is like any university. When the studying is over, with what they know now, they serve, and that's the return. There is an investment of knowledge in the School. When that knowledge produces benefits outside, that is the return.

Q: What do you mean by serve? What's servitude?

OSCAR: Servitude means to pass what you know to every other human being, because this knowledge belongs to all of humanity. In that sense, it is servitude in the great mystical way of servitude; it is our duty. Our primary duty as human beings is to see that our fellow human beings also get what we have. Because what we have is not only for us. That would be a totally egotistical and selfish way to see it, and it would be impossible for real knowledge to come to us if we have that attitude.

You only have real knowledge from the beginning if you have said to yourself that whatever you learn you are going in time to teach to somebody else. Because if you are learning just for yourself, the degree of *barakath* that comes to you is very small, is very little. Could be even nothing. The only way barakath flows is when you do understand that what you are taking is not for you, it's for everybody because it's a truth, an objective truth, and it's a law that it's for everybody. So you don't take for yourself, you take with the feeling that you are a channel. Then barakath flows. If you don't feel that you are a channel, that you are a container to be filled just for the sake of being filled, there is no flow.

When you need to change the liquid in a filled container, the old liquid must be drained. Then comes the new liquid, and even then if you stop, the new liquid in time becomes putrid. You have to continue and never stop. For us, this continual going is the servitude to others. So I say that we have to consider Arica as an investment of spiritual knowledge, of intellectual knowledge, of moral knowledge, and of physical knowledge. All this knowledge has to flow. And the investment is going to pay in these four levels.

Q: Are you speaking about teaching this knowledge in order to proselytize to people?

OSCAR: In Arica we don't proselytize because, well, we are not making a cult. This is not a cult. So we don't proselytize. It is the same as mathematics. With mathematics you don't proselytize. It is a knowledge that is indispensable. Exactly in the same way that mathematics is taught, we teach the methods of Arica. They are scientific, they are perfectly well measured, and so on.

Q: What are the results of the method?

OSCAR: The result is self-understanding, and if people

understand themselves and understand the society and so on, it means better relations, better conservation, better sense of direction; all that is improved because now the goals are clear. The goal is to have a better society. First, to be a better human being with your family, with your job, with society as a whole, more responsible.

The entire business of Arica could be synthesized in the work of really becoming responsible for the entire process of humanity. From the beginning in Arica we have said one thing. The highest moral problem that we propose from the beginning is to say that until human beings are responsible for the entire humanity, they are not yet completely responsible for themselves.

But this can't be just a declaration. It has to be factual. That means it has to be worked out. It is not a thing that we achieve just by saying, "From this moment, I am responsible for the entire humanity." For somebody that has not the level, it is just a slogan. A slogan has its own effect, no doubt, but self-hypnosis is not real.

Because, if somebody says in this very moment, "Well, the thing is to be responsible for the entire humanity"—fabulous. And if he immediately believes that he is responsible for the entire humanity, it is a total lie, because at that point he is not even responsible for himself. He didn't do the work that it is necessary to do for understanding ourselves. You know, one thing that has to be very clear is that understanding ourselves has been, since the beginning of time, the most difficult thing that a human being can do. It is the highest problem.

Nevertheless, it has always been taken for granted that since we are human beings we have it already. And it's not like that. It has to be achieved as a condition. So if you see, responsiblity is something that goes by degrees; it is not something that you have all at once.

Q: Is that what you mean when you say that in Arica we have been working so seriously steady?

OSCAR: What I was referring to there is that when something

is serious it always takes its own time. It is not spurious like a soap bubble with no consistency. So, what we are proving with a school that has been here for so much time, with so much effort, with so much sacrifice, and with so much steadiness and continuity, is that we are really sweating and working. With all the time that has passed, now we are not a new school, we are a school that has roots. We will be normally respected. We are people who work very hard, and at the same time there is no menace. There are no papers and no signatures. In Arica there is no compromise at all. It is totally free. You are there because you want to be there.

Q: What keeps the Aricans together?

OSCAR: The work is true. It is true and self-evident. For Aricans, that ties them together even through the hard time that we have had until now, because we were in the process of making a school. Now that the School is ready, it is different. We are ready to go outside as a school, a group of people that have the same qualities, characteristics, and the same goals, aim, unity of purpose, interaction, work, everything. Here school is meant in the same way that you would say a school of fishes, in the sense of a compact mass of individuals with the same purpose, the same way of being, the same charisma; they are equal, they are the same family. Now, in our case, we are a family. We are a family in the sense of metasociety. That is, for us, we are brothers and sisters, seriously. This is not an outside declaration; it's our family for sure. And, well, it has all the problems that any family has. The only difference is that we are a huge, immense family as never before, and it is going to become bigger and bigger. We know it. At the end, what we say is, respecting all the rest, humanity is going to understand itself so well that it is going to become one family.

A HISTORICAL MOVEMENT

Interview by Karimu Kudura, 1979

AT THE TIME of this interview, Karimu Kudura was publishing a journal called *Inside*, designed to stimulate discussion on aspects of Arica theory and their connection to the larger issues of politics and the future of the planet. Kudura asked Oscar to address himself to the destiny of America and the role that Arica would play in it.

Oscar observed that since the colonies of North America were founded in accord with the Divine Principles of Freedom and Equality, the nation had a mystical destiny from the start. North American society believed in "the chance and the possibility of a democratic process"—an inherited goal we become ever closer to achieving. With the diverse mixture of races and nationalities, too, evolving toward a harmonious balance, the United States holds the best chance of becoming a metasociety, or society in unity with a common goal. The ideas of Arica which could aid in effecting this transformation help give the movement its historical significance. What is of critical importance, however, as Oscar stresses in the talk which follows this interview, is the precise timing with which these ideas must be introduced. In such a delicate matter as this, timing could spell the difference between survival and extinction.

Karimu Kudura. "Interview with Oscar Ichazo." *Inside*. June, 1979.

KARIMU KUDURA: Why did you choose America as the place to establish the Arica School? Was there a mystical tradition in America?

OSCAR ICHAZO: Well, America is a result of humanity. There is a big difference between, let's say, North America (speaking about the United States, and in some ways Canada, but mainly the United States) and the rest of America, Latin America. Spanish and Portuguese America were developed for the benefit of the structure of the colonial system. In the case of Latin America it was serving mostly Spain and in another sense Portugal. All the production, all the benefits of Spanish America were entirely for the benefit of Spain. And obviously, you know, that led Latin America to become, let's say, *Spanish* America, a colony in complete servitude to the motherland.

The case of the United States was rather different because the colonies were founded with the idea of making a new country, so it started a step ahead of what was going on in Europe as a whole, and especially in England, where freedom and equality were becoming the main problems. So, you see, the founders of America were a mystical type of colonist who were coming here not to serve the motherland but to make a new country. So there is a difference, a big difference. The most important difference is that this country started with the good karma (if you want to put it that way) of making this place a place of freedom for religion. And from the freedom of religion came also individual freedom. So they were speaking of two things at the same time: they were speaking of 'communal freedom' in the sense that they could do whatever they thought was correct for achieving the goal of mysticism, and all that comes with that; and in the second degree, an 'individual freedom' beyond structure.

There is another very important thing: the independence of America. For the first time in the history of humanity there was a society that really believed in the chance and the possibility of a democratic process. Now, that democratic process couldn't start at the beginning of the Republic. That is not the way it was. It happened in a process, and we are still in the process of achieving that goal. We haven't achieved it completely, but there is no doubt that every year we are closer and closer to becoming a solid society with all the richness of the differences and, at the same time, the strength of a cohesive society that has the same goals, the same principles. And everybody is free to do and to achieve those principles or those goals in their own way. This is immensely important for humanity because it is the first case that we have as a country as a whole.

In America, because of the freedom of its society, there was a lack of heavy intellectual structures. In Europe, of course, those structures were already very, very old and very difficult to overcome and reform. So the reform in Europe came at a very slow pace in comparison to the United States. Now, I am not saying that there were not tough structures here; I am not saying that at all. They were very tough, but nevertheless, there is a Constitution. There is a structure of thought that really wanted to go beyond the problems, even now. So let's say that we have the 'cause', or we have the way for it. And it is a matter of time for the society to start understanding more and more its own responsibility to achieve those goals.

Then you see that for the first time we have, really, a technological society. With that I mean that we have a society which has different kinds of parameters, an unbelievable inter-communication. Communication transmits to us all that we support as main ideals, therefore, everything is at hand. We have television on most of the time. The media has risen so much that it makes almost all the country know everything at the same time. That really makes a tremendous difference. So we are living already in a society that is very coherent in ideas and very cohesive in its goals.

Now it is a matter of society developing more responsibility for the destiny of America, to be more clear about it. America is the society that is in this very moment closest to becoming a metasociety. That is, a society that is not only coherent in itself but also coheres for one purpose, with one 'going'. And because of that, its strength could exceed that of any past example. We must understand that in this very moment the United States generates a major proportion of the world's production of goods. It is really amazing; it is unbelievable.

So, you know, it becomes very obvious that in America something new is going to happen. It must be here, because there are all the elements for it. First, human elements: we have all the races in a very curious balance—I don't know how to put it better. That balance is increasing, is becoming more important day by day. The recognition is starting that in America diversity means richness.

And the Arica theory insists that the human race needs all its elements. Absolutely. We cannot believe that we are going to succeed in humanity if one of the parts of this entire body doesn't succeed at the same time. It would be a sick body. It would be like having trouble with the heart. Some of the main organs would not be functioning well. That means the entire body is sick and is not going to function properly. Now, America is really, in a way without wanting it, teaching the rest of the world just by example this importance and this richness. This produces a moral attitude, because in America theories that are fascist-like do not look like they will have a real chance. Here I don't want to go into politics; I'm just saying something that looks extraordinarily obvious.

We've got to see, you know, how much America has grown up since the thirties. We can speak about four main things that have caused this change: (1) the Depression, (2) World War II, (3) the Korean War, and (4) Vietnam. These four things have made America realize what its real position in the world is. And the position of America in the world is the position of a leader, want it or not, just by fact. And I repeat, want it or not. The dependence of all the rest of the planet on whatever is the course of America is so immense and so decisive that whatever we do here is going to have repercussions everywhere.

Q: Do we have any allies in this mission—other brothers and sisters in other approaches who are supporting the same mission?

OSCAR: Well, Arica has good relations with almost everybody. We are all doing the same thing, with different approaches. Most of the approaches that are around are very traditional and have been developed, some of them, thousands of years ago, and we cannot expect the reality of thousands of years ago to be the same as the reality we have now. Nevertheless, the main principles, the basic principles, are eternal principles and are the same in everybody.

What we see as differences are differences of approach, of method, of clarity of exposition, and finally, of discovering what we are. This is the main question. This question is an old question across the history of humanity, and we have references that it started before Socrates. In the Temple of Delphi (constructed in the fifth century B.C.), at the entrance, was written "Know Yourself."

Knowing what we are has been possible only across a kind of a leap—I don't know how better to say it. A leap. And in this case I am using the word 'leap' in the way that Kierkegaard employed it. He said that between the real world and the mystical world there is no bridge. And because there is no bridge, we've got to make the leap, a leap of faith. And once we have reached faith and understand the total, we *still* cannot explain it. Because faith is inexplicable. We say, however, that Arica has discovered the bridge and the bridge *can* be explained. That is our main difference.

Now, this effort is not only ours. It started long ago. You have all the works of Madame Blavatsky, all the works of the Theosophists around Blavatsky and Besant; you have the work of Alexandra David-Neel; you have the work of all the translations of the very blessed Lama Kazi Dawa-Samdup.

And before that, there was the tradition in Europe of the Teutonic Knights on one side; on the other side you had the Knights Templar; and you have the traditions of the alchemists which really started with Paracelsus. You have the traditions of the Martinists (we don't know exactly at what point the Martinists started), and with the Martinists there have been very important ones like Papus. They really spoke about alchemy in a very secretive way, only by oral transmission—also about the Tarot. They were very concerned about Tarot. Raymond Lully was the first really to speak about Tarot very clearly—as a 'machine of thinking' rather than for divination. There is the Expectant Church, only known in the high esoteric levels, the last Patriarch of which was the Viscount Leo Costet de Mascheville, with whom I worked.

And there are a lot of names it is very important to speak of. Prabhavananda Saraswati followed all the mysticism of Ramakrishna, and he was a very close disciple of Vivekananda. And my understanding is that he also worked with Swami Sivananda.

I also worked in the Tibetan tradition with the main four sects. Nevertheless, I worked more with the Drugpa, who are not really recognized like the main four sects. The four that are recognized are the Nyingmapa, the Sakyapa, the Kargyupa, and the Gelugpa. And they don't recognize the Drugpa. As for the Drugpa, you know, they don't recognize anybody. That's how they are. But the Drugpa are pretty big in Nepal and Mongolia.

I also worked with the Sufis, with most of the Sufi sects. There are other Sufi sects, not so well known, with whom I did not work, but they are not the main Sufi sects. The most important Sufi sects, no doubt, are the Suhrawardi, Chisti, Helveti, Naqshbandi, Rifai, Bektashi, and Mevlevi.

Q: Could you give us a little background about the enneagon?

OSCAR: About the enneagon, all that we have is a legend; we don't have historical data. But it is said that it is extremely old, extremely old. The first one who really spoke in a way about it was the Sixth Imam. He was the first in popularizing it, not inventing it. The enneagon was taken in a very secluded way; it was only given under very tough conditions of initiation after a long time of being in a sect, more than twenty years at least.

However, Gurdjieff had the mission of popularizing some of these ideas, which by the way, were already in Europe across the initiation of the Templars and of those who came in close relation with the mystical tradition of Islam, like St. Francis of Assisi and later Paracelsus.

Q: What do you mean when you say the 'wave' is our only ally?

OSCAR: You know, we are a *historical* movement. We are not a coincidence, we are not a group of somebodies saying, "Okay, let's start this, let's do this, it's nice." It has happened, so it is part of the historical process. Now when I say the 'wave', that is the moment that becomes, you know, the tough need of survival, and we are now in that tough need of survival.

And with that, I say that the most important thing is the unity of society. If we can achieve the unity of American society, *it is a fact* that we can come to the unity of the world. If we don't achieve the unity in the United States, *it is a fact* that it is not going to be achieved in the world. And in that sense, you know, we are in danger; that's one of the killers—disorganization.

Q: How much time would you say we have? You once gave a time scale for humanity to jump its level or disappear.

OSCAR: You know, after really consulting deeply in all that I have studied, it became very obvious that our timing was going to take about ten years. And that timing we started counting in 1973. That was the first year of counting. We've got to say 1983.

Now, what I am saying is this: it is not that I believe that in ten years we are going to change everything. That would be beautiful! But it is the deep realization—deep in the sense of kath feeling, gut feeling—that unity is needed and that the normal differences in such a huge society mean enrichment rather than problems and misunderstandings. And we are certainly close to accepting this self-evident premise. Because if we would be robot-like, everybody the same, that would mean in that very moment, history would stop. You know, there wouldn't be interaction and we wouldn't go anywhere. There is no interrelation; there is no new thing; there is no elasticity. We become very poor, and that would signify crisis and death for our society based primarily on the values of the individual.

Q: What do you see that Aricans need to work on as a body?

OSCAR: The Arica theory and practice focus their attention on self-observation. If we employ our methods of self-observation, everything becomes spiritual work. And self-observation means, above all, responsibility. You have self-responsibility, and self-observation is there. You are observing your acts and you are responsible for them. That is the main focus of the work.

Q: Is there an inner circle of the School?

OSCAR: Well, you know, in the School there is no doubt that there are degrees of trainings, but there are no inner circles. Level is a matter of achievement; it is completely open. We have to understand that our School is a really democratic one. And you have seen in all the process of the School we have never, never, ever been partial with anybody. That's a reality.

Q: Oscar, do you yourself get tired or frustrated with the process?

OSCAR: Well, every process has its own difficulties, you know. Perhaps what really has tired me above all is the waiting. Because precisely that type of waiting is historical timing, or if you want to put it another way, the timing is so crucial. It is so crucial because it has to take its own time, since reality is not a product of our invention. The same is true of every natural process. And we are not in an invented process, we are in a natural process.

You know, winter is not the natural time for flowers, but now we are in spring. This year is when we must communicate to the general public the truth that we have found about the human psyche, it's composition, and the laws which govern it. Here it is necessary to insist once more that reality is not a fruit of our subjectivity. When internal work has not been responsibly worked, you can find yourself believing that you create your world, and that is the self-deceit. So we say that for the work in our time, we need a huge body of people recognizing the laws of the psyche in concordance with the laws of nature. With this scientific approach we can deal with a world that precisely is the outcome of science.

A FIVE PERCENT CHANCE

A talk by Oscar Ichazo in Los Angeles, 1979

ON SEPTEMBER 27, 1979, Oscar Ichazo appeared at an informal gathering of the Arica community in Los Angeles. What follows are his remarks to the group.

OSCAR ICHAZO: This is not precisely a lecture. Rather, it is coming here and saying hello to you. In another sense, I feel the enormous connection that I have with every one of the Aricans, and every time we are together there is the spirit, the *barakath* which flows between us, obviously. So this is a real meeting of, let's say, internal connection and internal understanding.

One thing we must understand very clearly is that Arica is a mission. With mission I mean, and I have been saying this all along, that we are involved in a historical process, that we are not something that comes from nothing. Arica is a result of the times, a result in the sense that it fills a need. Now, when those kinds of needs approach, humanity doesn't accept them immediately.

On the contrary, it rejects the new type of thinking which, by the way, is the only solution for that time. Because it is 'jumping'—if you want to use that word—or is going beyond

---

Oscar Ichazo. "A fireside chat." *Inside*. January, 1980.

what traditionally is accepted, it is rejected. And it is not just a mental rejection; it is beyond that. It is fear of losing ground. That we must understand.

Now, every time that humanity needed to make a leap, there has been this kind of trouble, this kind of struggle. First the mission would appear in a school, a real school, with obvious answers for that need to make a leap. But at the same time people would not want to change. They are very much afraid of change, number one.

Number two, they are very afraid of losing certain prerogatives that have been acquired by time and which the new ideas are saying don't work anymore. Those old ideas are regressive ideas, and being regressive they will put the entire society in danger, a danger which sooner or later will have a solution and it could be a very bloody one.

So for not having a bloody solution, it is better to understand the conditions of the time and to spiritually, intellectually, emotionally, and of course, physically accept those conditions and change. What happens then is that society becomes better, much better, much more solid, much more brilliant.

Humanity has got to be considered as an organism—we have been saying that all along. It is not a new idea. It is an old idea with some variations. But we are very definitive in our proposition that this humanity is one organism, and it is an organism that has very precise stages of development. Before now humanity was like a child growing up. Now it is no longer a child. Now it's got to achieve total maturity. Total maturity signifies this: understanding each other in totality. That understanding each other in totality cannot be—and please understand me well—the fruit of goodwill. It is not enough. It only can be understood if we understand ourselves, our psyches. Then, understanding our psyches, we can understand the psyches of all humanity. Then the words "we are one" are not just a slogan; they are the truth that we are feeling in ourselves. Because repeating slogans is easy and dangerous.

What happens with Arica is this: It is the time, exactly the time, for ideas that can match our time and can really jump all the problems that we have ahead. Before humanity could have this chance, it could make mistakes, not for a long time, for a very short period of time. But during that period of time the mistakes would be corrected in the most bloody way. There would be religious wars, there would be massacres, there would be all kinds of things in all humanity, everywhere because we are one organism.

But now, in the time of our maturity, what happens is that we don't have that much time. If we don't understand what we have to do now, we are dead, and everybody knows it. Everybody knows it. How many chances do we have to survive on this planet as a species? I am a very optimistic fellow, *very* optimistic, *immensely* optimistic, and I say no more than five percent, and it's not a joke.

Now, the violence of the internal ideas of Arica that can transform this society and make it into a metasociety is something that we must go with carefully. Because these ideas are too striking. They are shocking; they are violent in the sense of very fast change. We cannot be so irresponsible as to just throw all that to a society which is not going to understand it immediately. This would create worse contradictions than the ones we have, and perhaps, instead of helping, we will lose that only five percent chance that we have.

So it is our responsibility to be careful, careful that every time we work the Arica method, we work it as we are saying we should work it. Variations in the method really produce different results, which afterwards are very difficult to correct, if not impossible. I say, "if not impossible" because the Arica ideas, once they hit the consciousness of anybody, are like fire. They stay there, and if they have been twisted, they are going to stay like that—twisted—and that you don't correct. So you create a fanaticism that is going to work against the truth sooner or later.

Now, we've got to understand this also: that all these kinds of things have to happen. I am very optimistic, and I say, well, more trouble must be for more joy. In reality it doesn't look like it, but it has a very positive side. It makes us more cautious, and instead of going in the blink of an eye, which we could, it is better to wait for the signals that are already written.

For understanding those signals, by the way, it is necessary to have been initiated by real transmission in those kinds of languages which have been called the secret Kaballah. If you don't know them, you cannot read the Kaballah. You don't know the language; you don't know the alphabet of the thing. People imagine things but they are not really reading what is inside. There is more than that in the secret Kaballah, the one that has never been written and has always been transmitted across very few human beings. Why? Because what is said there is so definitive, is so tremendous, that if you are not prepared during a whole lifetime for that, you can go crazy right there. I mean it. And craziness here means not a bad thing for that soul, it means a good thing. He just couldn't accept it; it was not for him. Otherwise, he could talk about that and make many more crazy. So you see, the wisdom of humanity also knows how to be, and to conserve its own secrets that *must* be secrets until the moment when that secrecy doesn't mean anything anymore. We are very close to that. We are seeing that every day.

One of the most common things to speak about is love. And speaking about love is like this: When you really love somebody you don't talk about it. You keep it a secret. Otherwise it is not true. You are making a trick with it. We cannot really give love in the real sense of love if we are not complete human beings, if we are human beings in process. What we are giving is not real love. For example, take children. They are obviously human beings, very complete, but they are in the process of growing up. Then their love is not really for giving something; on the contrary, it is for taking something. And that's normal. So you know, when I see people speaking about love, love, love, love, love, love, I see children wanting and I say, "This egg needs a little bit of salt."

Because it is such a human word and is so convincing,

we try to forget all these obvious dangers, and we just try it as it is. But, you know, and we all know very well, the worst crimes in humanity have been committed in the name of love. I don't know how else I can explain it. The final thing, the final justification is love. Give me any case in this very moment, and I will prove to you that they did it for that word, love. The worst crimes.

In Arica, precisely because we've got to be serious (it is not that we *want* to be serious—we *have* to be serious), we don't talk too much about love. We prefer to interrelate between us, one giving to the other, knowing many times that the negative process of our brother is a very good thing for us, though it makes us suffer, no doubt. But that suffering is also good for our evolution. We are talking about evolution, and if we talk about evolution it is certain that we are talking of real love because we are going to achieve the maturity of human beings. Then love is going to be a secure thing. Before, forget it. What we should do, then, is to relate between our processes in a very serious way, because it is sure enrichment.

There is another thing I have to say to you. Every time that a new idea appears which is going to reform humanity in one way or another, what happens is this: There are always groups of people more ready to receive this kind of truth than others. This is normal, not good, not bad, just normal. But what happens is that those who receive the truth first become desperate to transmit that truth to everybody. Normally they get hit by everybody in the worst way. They are despised, and people say they are crazy, and this and that, and of course they start feeling threatened in their own convictions. So we also have to be more prudent, because we are in a time for not losing.

I used to say, at the beginning of the School, that fortunately we are not going to be thrown to the lions because, by the way, there are not too many lions in the world now. In another sense, there are things that are more frightening than lions, and they are imitation and direct bad will, which we have had to count on from the very beginning. And we did. Of course we had our part of all that, but the bad effects against Arica have been minimal, really minimal. In that sense, I guess, we did it brilliantly because the School really has had the necessary resistance to continue going and continue going, so many times waiting for the real movement.

I know how hard it is to wait. I don't like to wait. Who likes it? So many times I have said, "No, we've got to go now." The consequences have been very immediate for me: I have gotten sick. It's like I've been stopped, and stopped seriously, very seriously.

So you see, as human beings we are learning permanently. We are in a process of learning, even at the top. A human life is that, a process of learning. It is going to be a process of learning from the beginning to the end for all human beings.

What we have to do is to continue to be Aricans, very cohesive between us. Now we are going to start coming out with more trainings which are easier to participate in. The ideas of Arica are already everywhere. So it is the right time. We are not going to have bad shocks; on the contrary, I expect that we will be better received than before. Look at the spiritual movement. It is really decreasing badly. It is not like it was at the beginning of the seventies, and that is saying something. It means that the claims that attracted people don't attract them anymore. People want results, things that work, and that work *now*. That is one thing.

The other thing is this: This society, more than anything, knows that it needs instruments to change, and that it is good to change. Before, nobody wanted that. Even now there are many, many points that are still very tough, *very* tough, but very soon those points are going to start getting softer, because reality is telling us that we should change, and that we had better do it, the sooner the better.

Yet we have to wait for the right moment. We are going to start with our trainings which are easier to understand, not so internal as the trainings that we used to have. Now we want to release trainings that are more acceptable to the general public, and from that, those who want to can come to the more internal work of Arica which, of course, exists. We are going to do that, and really soon.

Now I have been very, very concerned to put a date. So many times I have said *then* it is going to happen, soon; and we do it, we do it, we do it, and it didn't happen. Now, I know that it is going to happen *soon*, and please just take my word.

I AM THE ROOT OF A NEW TRADITION

Interview by Dorothy De Christopher, 1981

WITH A BIOGRAPHY reminiscent of the life and travels of Gurdjieff, Oscar Ichazo is indeed a remarkable man. Though small-boned and of delicate appearance, he is a dynamic intellect and visionary and a force not to be taken lightly. Is enlightenment something elusive, ephemeral, a blessing to be prayed for, or is it something which one can plan for, work at, almost 'engineer'? Oscar claims the latter and ten years ago founded the Arica Institute to prove it. From its small beginnings in the desert of Chile where the first training with about fifty determined Americans was held, Arica has grown into an impressive and well-organized school of practical and esoteric mysticism. Over 200,000 people have taken advantage of at least one of Arica's wide variety of trainings, courses or workshops, developed to lead one on a nine-stage path toward enlightenment.

Oscar's vision includes the coming of a 'metasociety', a world of transformed institutions where people live for the common good. As he spoke of his sincere concern to graduate numbers of clearer individuals to serve the world, I saw a planet hanging in a balance where each heart must make the choice and decide the course our world will take.

Dorothy De Christopher. "I am the root of a new tradition." reprinted with permission from *The Movement Newspaper*. May, 1981.

DOROTHY DE CHRISTOPHER: In creating the Arica School, you have combined mysticism, ancient wisdom, and your experience, as the groundwork for the study of the development of human consciousness. You must have had some personal experiences with higher states that caused you to begin your exploration of the consciousness beyond the material planes.

OSCAR ICHAZO: When I was six years old, I started having serious periodic cataleptic attacks. Every two or three days, at the moment of sleep, I would become quite rigid and very frightened. It continued for many years.

At the beginning I was deadly panicked, but after the panic, I became cynical and after the cynicism, I felt "so what." I was living my life dying every day, and this went on for years. It put me in a very strange space. I was always a bit weird, and was not happy.

I felt tortured and the only way I found I could discharge my preoccupation was to try to find out about my sickness by reading everything I could. I made a really professional study until I finally found they didn't know anything about what I had. I can remember how outraged I was—I was quite furious for months.

Q: At what point did you find something which aided you in your quest to get well and understand what was wrong with you?

OSCAR: I was about thirteen years old and living in Bolivia at that time. The *curanderos*, or Indian medicine men, were very popular but nobody would take them seriously unless they were in a desperate situation. Sometimes their cures worked, sometimes they didn't. I started believing that there was something there, so I made friends with them and they finally gave me drugs. *Ayahuasca (yaje)* was my first drug experience. It's a vine which grows around trees and is found in the Amazonian forests.

Q: With your cynicism, what led you to believe their brand of ministration would work, and did it help you?

OSCAR: Well, at first everything they would tell me to do would work in certain, funny ways. I was very realistic and cynical at the time. I didn't believe in God, idolatry, or mysticism. For me, I was engaging in scientific research, and I thought that perhaps they had some medicines that people needed to know about. No more than that.

I was not considering anything mystical, but the ayahuasca gave me the tune and the scent that there was something else. In more than one of those ayahuasca experiences I was really led out of the body. It felt like a real experience, though I could have dreamt it—I'm not going to swear to it.

Q: When you had these out-of-the-body experiences in the mountains, did you see anything or feel anything which you remembered in the waking state?

OSCAR: Yes. It taught me many different things, but the most important was that everything in the universe is really only one thing. There was a perfect unity which had degrees of manifestation, with human beings at the top, no doubt. It was tremendous for me to experience the unity of matter, which is explained only intellectually in modern mathematics, not as a vital experience.

Q: Was this experience of unity a turning point in your life?

OSCAR: Well, one thing takes you to the next. I was already practicing yoga and had also played with hypnosis. I had investigated what we called 'banana' groups which studied Western and native Indian witchcraft and spiritualism. I had also looked into Theosophy and Hindu philosophy.

By the time I was nineteen, I was through with all that, and had the good fortune to meet an older man who took some interest in me, though at the time I didn't know why. This was around 1950, and this man invited me to Buenos Aires, where I was involved with a group of mystics, many of whom were seventy or eighty years old when I met them. I mostly just observed and was careful to be very quiet. I served them coffee, and I continued my friendship with many of them until they died.

Q: So here you had your first real sniff of authentic Eastern and Western mysticism?

OSCAR: Yes. I met some swamis who came around and gave initiations. I saw all types of yoga possible. We did a lot of tantra, both Indian and Tibetan. Later I repeated these studies in the Orient, but there I got the basis of it. It was mostly *kriya* yoga and a lot of the Kaballah. Whatever they talked about I would do, and sometimes when they had time they would teach me something and I learned very fast.

Q: This seems to have been an extraordinary experience—one house where many spiritual teachers passed through to share their knowledge. Were you the only student?

OSCAR: Well, they didn't view me as a student. The idea of these people with knowledge meeting to try to bring that knowledge together was originated somehow by Gurdjieff, but this is something that was insinuated rather than said.

Q: Were these teachers South Americans?

OSCAR: None of them was South American. They were Europeans or from the Middle East.

Q: Where did your travels take you after your association with the teachers in Buenos Aires? To the East?

OSCAR: I went to Santiago and started groups there in 1956, 1958, and 1960. During each of these groups I took a journey to the East.

Q: Did you go with your students?

OSCAR: No, alone. It was a difficult period because I was exiled from my country as a politician. They didn't want me there and it was difficult to travel, though I managed to get a passport and traveled anyhow.

Q: Where in the East did you study?

OSCAR: I studied tantra in the northern part of Kashmir and in the south of Iran, and Sufism in the Pamir.

Q: Where is the Pamir?

OSCAR: It is a plateau in Tadzhikistan near Afghanistan where there are missiles now. It is no longer accessible to people. At that time though, the Pamir was desolate. It is a very strange place because all the cultures of the East, through the Pamir, have some going toward the West. Tamerlane,

Ghengis Khan, all the invasions and all the communications between the Chinese culture and the Indian culture come from the Kashmir and the Pamir.

Today part of it is in the U.S.S.R. and China. There used to be three houses called "the monastery" there, but they have disappeared, I think. There was real knowledge taught there.

Padmasambhava, the founder of Tibetan Buddhism, came from the Pamir, and if you examine the theories of Padmasambhava, you will see that it's very close to that of the Sufi and Zoroastrian traditions.

Q: On your first trip you studied Sufism. Could you tell us about that?

OSCAR: The first Sufis I met were a school of Suhrawardis in Qandahar. And from there I made contact with Bektashis and Naqshbandis, and in Kabul, I made contact with what is called the Jemaluddin, the inner essence of the Muslim tradition. They assisted me with my trip to the Pamir, which was a very dangerous and crazy trip.

Q: Wasn't it by mule?

OSCAR: Yes, by mule, and really dangerous. When you are young you do those things.

Q: Did you go further East?

OSCAR: On the third trip I went to Hong Kong, which was a very important place for me because I really wanted to achieve a mastery of the Chinese classics. Since I couldn't go to mainland China, the closest place was Hong Kong, and I really learned much more than what I had set out to learn.

I became deeply involved in the Muslim, Indian, Japanese, and Chinese cultures. I already had very deep roots for that because I had been studying martial arts from the age of nine with Sensei Kentaro Ohara, a real samurai. And I had been involved in zazen and hatha yoga.

Q: When you came back from the East, you spent a few years processing what you had learned. Could you tell us about that?

OSCAR: When I came back in 1960, I started teaching my study group again. Then in 1964, I went to my father's house in Bolivia to spend a year in solitude. I had an experience there that came without my effort and really surprised me. I felt that this experience was *it*—that I didn't need to learn anything else. I had reached the totality.

Q: Is what you're describing what you have called a "divine coma"?

OSCAR: It's ordinarily known as a coma, but also was a state of ecstasy. My body was in a very mild state of being asleep, but I was not asleep—I was completely conscious. All the body functions diminished so intensely that for moments I lost the reality that I was living. I experienced living not only this reality, but other realities at the same time. I had many visions, one after the other, which, when I was in that state, made tremendous sense. But when I went out of that state I started having my doubts.

Q: What kinds of visions did you experience?

OSCAR: I saw how the laws have organized the cosmos itself, laws that I had already understood rationally, but now which I was *seeing*. I had experiences of cosmology, of how the world was created. I would see the mathematical relationships between things, which put me on the track of a new calculus. This calculus dealt with logical problems themselves rather than translating them to a different language as we do now.

Another type of experience was seeing what type of a time we are in now and what is needed to be done to give solutions to this troubled world we live in. During that time, the early sixties, few people were aware that we were so close to trouble. On the contrary, there was an expectancy that we would move forward endlessly. In the visions I had, I saw the entire planet approaching certain collapse, the kind of collapse a physical body has due to sickness, deterioration, internal contradictions. It was really seeing humanity dying.

Q: Would you describe this experience as enlightenment?

OSCAR: Oh, definitely. But, you know, enlightenment is something which has internal degrees also. It's not something you achieve all at once. The first enlightenment is to be completely aware that the entire game of our life is consciousness. That is *kensho*—when you are aware that consciousness is the thing to focus on and not the mind.

While the mind is composed of thoughts, feelings and sensations, consciousness has no components at all. Our consciousness is the source of the mind. If the consciousness is unclear or is suffering, our mind is going to be unclear and suffer. We do not control our mind until we have our consciousness clear.

Q: That's interesting, because many seekers and paths work on the assumption that if the mind could be stilled, then consciousness would manifest and clarity would be present. Yet you speak of the consciousness as suffering.

OSCAR: Let's put it this way. Our entire manifestation is nothing but consciousness. Our body is a manifestation of that consciousness and can suffer; our emotions are a manifestation of that consciousness and can suffer; our mind is a manifestation of that consciousness and can suffer. If that consciousness itself is not liberated, it suffers.

Gurdjieff said rather than helping yourself, try to help God. That seems bizarre—how is anybody going to help God? However, the central idea Gurdjieff was communicating was that the part of God that is in us is suffering, and if we stop suffering we really help God. If everything is an emanation of God, it has to return to the source. The entire creation and human life is really that effort from the blessing of God in his creation to return to Himself.

Q: How would you describe or define what you understand as God?

OSCAR: It's impossible to qualify or define God. Suppose you speak with a Buddhist. He will say God doesn't exist, yet there are subtleties here. What he really means is that God is beyond existence, and that 'beyond existence' cannot be qualified because we don't know what it is. We'll never know.

If a person sees the manifestations of the divine and he

obviously experiences all those manifestations, then he has security of the existence of God. In that unqualified term which we don't have for Him, we just know God 'is'.

What we have of God is just the result, not Himself. We'll never have that. That is why creation has only one Creator and the Creator Himself has only that quality. If He had any other quality, He wouldn't be the Creator—He would be created.

You know, I always laugh a lot, with all due respect, when I hear mystical people discussing these things. It is as Gurdjieff used to say, it's like trying to put the 'empty' into the void. *(laughter)*

Q: After that one striking experience, have you continued having them? Is there a sense that your enlightenment deepens as time goes on?

OSCAR: That was, for me, the peak experience. It's one thing to be in that moment of pure light and quite another when you 'come down' and see yourself. At the time, I thought that I was going to be a very happy man just living my experience and writing books. I thought I had everything in order. Yet at the end of the experience, there was a sense that I had a duty to teach all that, and I honestly didn't like the idea.

Q: There was a sense of a mission?

OSCAR: Yes, like I was really commanded to do it.

Q: The techniques you teach are as varied as your background. Did you find the basis for the *Nine Ways of Zhikr* training in studying with Sufi sects in the East?

OSCAR: I had been working with different types of *zhikrs* much before I went to the East. The Arica way of zhikr is more powerful than the type of zhikr done by Sufi sects because it includes all nine ways of doing zhikr.

The most powerful type of zhikr can take you to a state of ecstasy in which you lose the sense of yourself as a separate being and melt into the universal. It's the moment when you make the connection with the divine. It is necessary to have a guide who really knows the technique deeply; otherwise it is very confusing and can even be dangerous.

The 'path' starts in a person the moment that person becomes clearly aware that he is dying. Normal life is that which exhausts itself and is like dying without awareness. Jesus said very clearly that if you want to win your life you are going to lose it, and if you lose your life you are going to win it.

The real way is to live a totally normal life at the same time you are living a divine life. That is, consecrate every act you do so that you are not doing for yourself, but you are doing with an extra purpose which is beyond yourself, transcendental to yourself. Then it's going to have real value.

By going beyond ourselves we can evolve our internal structures. We cannot do that if first we are not clear about our physical being and how it works. Our physical being is structured for covering outside needs, not inside needs. So the inside needs are something we have to work for.

Q: Why don't more people choose the inner path?

OSCAR: People are completely preoccupied with the outside world. They don't even imagine that an internal world exists. Their minds go around serving outer intentions and never serving the inner intentions, which are those that are going to stay with them.

Happiness is something that does not exist at the physical level. People are just consumed by things. What we call entertainment is just that—sitting down in front of the television and having your energy sucked out in a way that you feel you are living. In reality you are actually dying.

All the paths which say that it is spiritual to become yourself and to tune into yourself are completely a mistake, because this is like getting inside a shell. You are separating yourself from the universal energy.

Q: What must we do then?

OSCAR: If we start believing that we are the cause of our own world, we are totally mistaken since we don't create anything—not even our dreams. We have to hold down our egoistic cravings. Instead of serving ourselves, we must start serving what is higher than us, from whence we come, because we all come from Humanity. We owe everything to Humanity.

If we take ourselves seriously in the sense that we are the center, we are being egoistical. In the mystical tradition, this is called Satan. Satan is that which denies the interior path in us.

It is important not to be tempted by our own demon, our ego. Our ego is just the entire spectrum of our lacks. In trying to fulfill those lacks, we lose our life.

If we become aware that those lacks do not in reality exist and are just part of a personal process, then we can go beyond those lacks and become integrated in ourselves. Then we can be useful for the common evolution.

Q: So the purposes of Arica are for each student to establish himself or herself firmly in their inner life and also in universal service?

OSCAR: The first thing is to know exactly how your psyche works. Then you can rule yourself and direct yourself wherever you want.

Your efforts have value only if they have the necessary energy behind them. You can make a thousand efforts and they will yield you nothing. On the other hand, it's possible to make only one effort with the necessary energy and it will affect you permanently. It's a matter of knowing.

That is why real transmission is very important in all traditions. I have received many top-level transmissions, and in addition to that I have elaborated a different system. I am the root of a new tradition, or a new path, which in essence has come as a consequence of the other paths, but which is also different because it has different elements, more accurate explanations for our psyche.

Never before has the human psyche been described using the methods I propose. Never before has it been possible almost to engineer your own path. This word 'engineer' might be repulsive to someone who is mystical, because in mysticism things which go along with reason are not only unacceptable, but seem contradictory.

That is because until now there was no logic that could grasp unity, and so reason has been thought to be opposed to the spiritual path. If we have a logic with which we can grasp unity, then our reason and the path become one. That makes the spiritual path more independent and, in a sense, more democratic. Before, the master or teacher relationship was necessary. Once all the rules of the game have been discovered, who needs the master or the teacher?

Q: Could you comment on the paradox of enlightenment as something prepared extensively for, or in your terms "engineered," yet at the same time, a blessing, a dispensation, something which cannot be controlled or manipulated. Isn't enlightenment a gift from God?

OSCAR: Before, enlightenment was something of a coincidence. The parameters and variables were tuned in such a way that you couldn't determine when, how, and if such a thing would take place. It just happened. That was because we didn't know exactly what the architecture and structure of the psyche was.

Now that we know, we can do it. In medicine, before we knew exactly what the causes of illnesses were, you either had a miracle cure or perhaps died. Today we can relatively predict the duration of an illness and cure it.

Spiritually we can be more accurate than with the physical plane, so you can really engineer yourself better. Once you know, you can connect yourself with different types of energy we have only dreamt of.

Mystical work until now has been personal work, individual work. Arica proposes a social path. That is the big difference. Until now the path has been a path of coincidences. Now we can employ a system which has been tested and works. The proof is the School.

But I want more than that. I want more scientific research.

When we do 'tuning', that is, when everybody meditates at the same time, the results are fantastic. The next day people's faces are different. The results are much faster, to the extent that if you speak of the traditional paths as a horse, Arica is a jet.

Q: Would you recommend the many path approach or choosing one path and going all the way with it for one who is seeking enlightenment?

OSCAR: Every practice, in reality is okay. Everything has its own validity. I would say that in our time we have to produce something stronger than what we already have. Every period of time in history has its own needs and its own problems. Each age has a new technology and the instruments get more refined, more specific.

Our time requires not only new instruments, but new techniques which deal with this age. That is what Arica is all about. The way to deal with this is first with a new logic, one that deals with unity, and one that projects a new mathematics, clear and complete. It's possible to have a new atomic theory and a complete revision of how we think about biology.

Our physical world has to be seen differently. We are still seeing with eyes of two centuries ago. We are behind our times, which is a dangerous situation.

It's a matter of discovering the techniques of how to evolve and how to conduct ourselves in a mature and totally independent way. I'm not going to say anything against religion, but man should depend on his own condition, abilities, and qualities for his mysticism.

People working together in a group progress so fast that it is almost inconceivable. You can realize yourself with such speed when you start doing exercises in a group, that a week becomes like years for you.

Q: Could you talk about the age-old contradiction of needing a teacher as a guide to the uncharted realms, but also needing to find enlightenment within yourself where no one can go with you? How does the Arica system approach this seeming problem?

OSCAR: Arica offers a sharp scientific description of the psyche and what you can expect. On the other hand, the mystical part of Arica does need to be validated, although the need for this is much less in Arica. We don't have rules; we don't say "do this" or "don't do this," because we feel that the entire path is a matter of responsibility rather than discipline. There's nothing wrong with discipline, but it has to come from inner responsibilities.

You really have to choose and take upon yourself the responsibility of *doing* the path. Nobody can do for you that which you have to do. One difference between Arica and other mystical paths is that normally the teacher takes your karma. But that is very relative, because in the final analysis, only you can live your life.

Q: In your system a student can work through many of the stages without needing a teacher monitoring his specific inner progress. At what point does work with a teacher, or yourself, begin?

OSCAR: When you start in Arica, from the very beginning you can feel the energy that we call the 'energy of the School'. This is very real. You start receiving an extra energy that you didn't have before.

Q: You mean that newcomers can tap into a 'pool' of energy resulting from the earlier students' having processed a lot?

OSCAR: Exactly. In every mystical idea, a center that radiates that type of energy must be created. It starts on a small scale and then grows. The pioneers who take the responsibility at the beginning are the ones who are going to sweat more. They open the road, which means building the road, which takes a lot of effort. It's an effort that spiritually has immense compensation.

The teacher comes in, more or less, in the eighth or ninth level of the School. The teacher becomes actually indispensable while working with the astral, mental, and causal bodies; this means telepathy.

At this stage, the main thing that a student feels is the reversing of the attitude about his world. What we call the waking state becomes the dream state and what we call the dream state becomes the waking state. A student becomes aware of different spaces and different realities which are more real than this reality. In making this transition, a student really needs a guide who has been there and is an expert.

Q: If a student went through the whole Arica system and completed the various stages, would he have experienced enlightenment?

OSCAR: Yes, remembering that enlightenment is something which comes in several stages and degrees. It means to feel consciousness as being the root of our life, our existence, everything.

There comes a moment when you discover that consciousness doesn't move, has not been created, and is not going to be split, collapse or be destroyed. It is an external principle that has no conditions and is beyond existence.

Arica is a social movement rather than a personal movement. When you work in Arica, you do work on yourself but the results are going to benefit the School as a whole. At a point, the School reverses that energy to you—you give one and you are going to receive one hundred. It's a very good deal.

We're speaking on spiritual terms because materially speaking we don't bother. Your attitude and intention is what counts. You give love to your brothers and sisters in the School and you receive love and caring. Everybody knows intuitively who is giving and who is not giving.

And in Arica we encourage curiosity. If someone wants to visit another master, another path, we don't oppose it because if he benefits, he will benefit the School. If the other path is better for him, that's okay too. Our doors are never closed and he can come back at a later time if he wants to.

Q: So through the Arica School you have set down in black and white the complete road map to the psyche and the human developmental process?

OSCAR: Yes, and it works in every case and in all cases. Now I wish to go more public. I'm writing the books one by one, once and for all. I have waited a long time until I felt it was the right moment.

I have to say that not everything is intentional on my part and for one reason or another I could never put all the material in order. The road maps are in order, or I wouldn't have started teaching, but I have to describe things in a way that the general public can read and understand. It's one thing to work personally with people. You can explain things in mystical terms that the general public wouldn't accept.

Q: Could you describe in simple terms the basis of the Arica teachings?

OSCAR: The first question is, What is the root of life? What makes us feel that we are alive? We've got to define that. I say that what makes us feel alive are the instincts.

And what is an instinct? I define instincts as living questions which we don't ask ourselves, but nevertheless are there. There are three fundamental questions. The first one is, How am I?—Am I okay or not?

The second question is, Who am I with? This is our relation instinct. You've got to know how you are and whom you are with. In the animal kingdom if an animal doesn't know who it is with, it is going to die immediately. If I am a gazelle about to make friends with a jaguar, I am not going to survive.

The third question is, Where am I? The moment you don't know where you are you go into panic. We cannot lose that question; we've got to know where we are all the time. Each one of the instincts evolves into a kind of entity which is independent unto itself.

Q: Is this part of what you call the basic enneagon of the psyche?

OSCAR: Yes. This is the enneagon of the nine *hypergnostic*

systems which manifest in these three instincts, the four functions—space, time, expression, and coordination—and the two poles which close the circle—the sexual and the spiritual. This is the first level of study.

Q: Is this similar to Gurdjieff's enneagram?

OSCAR: I found the enneagon before reading Gurdjieff. It had tremendous impact on me. I was very curious about it and constantly asked, "What is this?" Finally one of my teachers in Afghanistan said to me, "Look, don't try to understand that, because the person who understands that is going to explain it to everyone." *(laughter)*

Suddenly, I started explaining this to him point by point, and it was correct. When I started seeing inside the enneagon, I perceived things that they were not seeing.

Q: The number nine seems to be important in your teachings.

OSCAR: Every manifestation can be divided into nine points —anything.

Q: What are the 'domains'?

OSCAR: In the second level of study, the student works with the nine systems as the psychic projection of the domains of consciousness. The domains are projected in our psyche and in our surrounding world.

Arica says that our psyche is a projection of our body, and our body is the fruit of our consciousness. Hence consciousness is previous to the body. It is what makes our body.

Consciousness is composed of nine domains. There are nine systems in our body which give us the impression of the nine domains of consciousness. We know that we have eight senses—hearing, smell, equilibrium, touch, taste, kinesthetic, temperature, and sight—which give us the impression of the energies coming from the outside.

The eight energies crossing the eight senses give us eight consciousnesses, which all together make the ninth consciousness. That is the consciousness of life. Without these eight consciousnesses, unity, the ninth, would be impossible.

Q: Is the Arica work also divided into nine?

OSCAR: Yes.

Q: And the first stage is the *40-Day Training*?

OSCAR: Yes. Then comes the *Domains* training and another training, *Protoanalysis*. Those are followed by *Psychoalchemy, Opening the Rainbow Eye,* and after that, the *Alpha Heat* ritual. Then comes *The Cutting of the Adamantine Pyramid.* Number eight we call *The Opening of the Golden Eye,* and the final training really is the understanding of the cosmic psyche, not as an individual expression, but as a universal expression. We call this stage *The Monastery* for lack of a better name.

Q: How does a student begin working with the diagram of the enneagon?

OSCAR: He doesn't work alone with the diagram. We go along system by system and the student reviews his life experiences, seeing them from a neutral point of view rather than identifying with those experiences and processes. Understanding the systems means understanding how you are composed internally. These same systems are then employed with application to the external world.

Q: And these are the domains?

OSCAR: Yes. You could call working with the systems a complete physical stage. You could call the domains emotional because they are tied with relationships. Now you need to put both together in order to become independent of the systems and of the domains.

For that we do *Protoanalysis*, the third stage. This is where you really work with the 'fixations'. Then you start seeing how you are continually making a circle without being aware of it.

Q: And the fixation is where a person is stuck, the pivotal point of their 'dilemmas'?

OSCAR: Yes. Everything you start in life, you start from there.

Q: Once knowing my dilemma, my fixation, how do I get unstuck?

OSCAR: By just recognizing it. In the moment you recognize that you have this mechanism going and you see the mechanism, it becomes pretty funny. You begin to see that your internal processes are not that monumental, and that you can handle them.

Q: Does the student work with other techniques during this recognition process, like meditation?

OSCAR: Yes. We call them techniques of support because at the same time a student is working on the outer mechanism, it's necessary to start sharpening up what we have inside. One of the main things to train yourself in, no doubt, is meditation, but meditation is not the only thing.

Q: What's the next stage?

OSCAR: *Psychoalchemy.* That consists of learning how to transmute normal energy into superior energy. One of the techniques we use is *Kinerhythm*. People are shown how to be very observant while doing a series of very precise kinesthetic movements very slowly.

Q: There's one very interesting technique in which you work with what are called yantras. Could you tell us about that?

OSCAR: The yantras are really visual mantras. Both mantras and yantras are tools for concentration for meditation. The idea is that if you concentrate on specific types of sounds and forms, you can tune yourself to your interior. It is a key which not only opens the internal self, but also tunes us with higher consciousness and higher entities.

Q: Arica seems imbued with such a positive attitude and geared toward the realization of a unified world at a time when prophets of doom spread tales of catastrophes. Could you address yourself to this?

OSCAR: You go beyond catastrophe when you confront it eye-to-eye like a true warrior. A warrior will not have a war if he takes a cold look at war and its difficulties. And a warrior is not a man of guts—he's a man who knows if he runs from the difficulties, those difficulties will persecute him and kill him.

If the world doesn't want a catastrophe we must face the

dangers, and one of the worst dangers we are facing is that the climate is going to change. The ionosphere has been hurt, and the danger is that climatic change not only threatens our outside being, but produces a change of all organic manifestation on our planet.

The more aware humanity is as to the danger of sure extinction, the more our possibilities of survival. If we deny the possibility that humanity can be a casualty, we are putting ourselves in a situation of blindness that could be dangerous.

Q: This awareness could cause many people to focus on the negative. Wouldn't that feed it instead of helping?

OSCAR: One person on the good side is equal to a million on the other side. The majority isn't needed for the balance. One carat of a diamond is equivalent to several tons of sand. There is an immense difference between an aware person and the rest.

Q: On the spiritual level, when you look at the spiritual community in this country, are you hopeful?

OSCAR: Yes. Everybody is doing his part in one way or another. Since about 1971, it started like a rush. All types of traditions have appeared here and that's a blessing, and yet these ancient traditions have already said everything they have to say. We need something that belongs entirely to our times.

Being modern means being absolutely and radically different. If we are not capable of coming up with something totally new, from a different direction, we are not going to make it.

A serious movement, not under the spell of fanaticism or dogma, must be created with truth that is understandable, truth that we can grasp and measure. It has to be a large circle of people because it is a big, big job.

Q: Is this what you mean by the term 'metasociety'?

OSCAR: Metasociety really means a transcendental society in which one is not living for the individual but is living for humanity as a whole. Until now, society has served the individual. I'm not saying that now we have to serve society, because that goes with socialist ideas, and both socialism and capitalism are idealistic.

Either we become a metasociety very soon or we die. We must not believe that the metasociety is going to be a 'disco party', and that everybody is immediately going to be blissed out. Metasociety really starts when we become aware that our internal possibilities are much better than our external ones. The external ones have always led us to suffering—craving, compromise, loss of freedom, and loss of self in all possible ways.

The worst way of losing our self is believing that we are the masters of our own world. That is not so. The laws are the masters of our lives and we can only deal with our lives when we know the laws. It is said by all traditions that at the end of time these negative forces, the ego forces, are going to be very strong.

Q: Do you see the world in this type of polarization right now?

OSCAR: Yes indeed, and it's absolutely necessary. It's not wrong. Opportunism comes at the same time as the truth. It is going to dress itself in the same clothes as the truth.

Truth has always been rejected throughout history. It becomes difficult to say what is true and what is not true, but the difference is that the opportunist has no roots and must imitate the truth.

Q: Will we then grasp the truth this time instead of rejecting it?

OSCAR: We'd better, because this is the last crisis. If we don't, we're dead.

Q: Ten years ago you started the Arica system and worked with it closely for five years. In the last five years you have not been personally involved. How, besides graduating numbers of 'aware' people, have you been working toward balancing the crisis in the last five years?

OSCAR: One part of the effort has been very internal—

taking the negativity that has been around into myself. I have been absorbing it and transmuting it in a spiritual way. It's very difficult work. Fortunately, the worst part is over. Now, I feel we are going to go very fast.

Q: You have given us what you describe as the complete road map, the complete parameters for the human psyche. There are just so many energies, so many functions, domains, illusions—exactly these many and no more. It's hard for me to think in terms of these strict limits.

OSCAR: Historically speaking, we can say that we 'know' something when we understand its limits. Before we discovered that our planet was round and had limits, we believed we were surrounded by a limitless ocean. We ignored our physical environment because we didn't know the limits. Once a limit appears, we have the possibility of understanding. Until then, we only have beliefs, ideas, and dogmas because our mind has to work with something. Where we don't have a reason which goes along with empirical reality, we need a dogma to support our mind's functioning. Once the limit is discovered, arguments are over. The world is round and that's that. Nobody can argue that it's flat just because he sees flat.

In the same way, in the spiritual area, the last area we are going to know because it is the highest, we are going to reach the point where spirit has limits, where spirit is material. It's a different type of matter, but material anyhow.

So, if spirit is material, it has limits. And once we have grasped its limits, we are going to understand what spirit is. Before now, only those few who have reached very high states have known these limits. They have been very few and once there they cannot talk about it and explain it because they don't have the language and the science.

What I am proposing is simply this: to explain precisely what hasn't been explained up till now. What is needed is a group of scientists thinking in the spiritual way. Then society will be nourished by these ideas and start living them culturally rather than intellectually. Once the entire mechanism of the psyche is exposed, people will see that all the real traditions, all the real paths, go to the same place.

THE CHALLENGE TO CHANGE

Interview by Alfie Fox, 1981

IN AUGUST, 1981 Oscar delivered his first public lectures since the *Kensho* lectures of 1976, entitled *Between Metaphysics and Protoanalysis, A Theory for Analyzing the Human Psyche*. He first lectured to a thousand people at Lincoln Center's Alice Tully Hall in New York, then traveled to Maui, Hawaii, where he gave a modified version of the lecture, and he completed his tour during September in the United Kingdom, where he delivered a third form of the lecture at the Collegiate Theatre in London.

This interview was conducted in London shortly after his lecture there. Alfie Fox, a British journalist and broadcaster, addressed himself to issues and topics raised in the lecture and in informal discussions during Oscar's visit.

ALFIE FOX: Mr. Ichazo, for several years now you have been developing a method which you say could lead man away from the threat of extinction and towards the realization of his true capabilities and purpose. How real is the threat of extinction?

OSCAR ICHAZO: Well, it's common knowledge everywhere that the threat of the extinction of humanity is a very cruel reality. It's impossible for us to believe that we are going to survive a nuclear holocaust or even a partial holocaust, because that is totally out of the point. Every time that we produce such a gigantic explosion of radiation, we cremate, so to speak, not only the biosphere with the explosion itself, but even worse, you know, is the consequence in the ionosphere. The radiation really destroys ions in the sense that it destroys the entire shield that we have against cosmic rays and that transforms cosmic rays into beneficial ions. Without the ionosphere, we have the cosmic radiation burning the naked biosphere, and frying the biosphere, and we live in the biosphere, no?

But, you know, the problem is one of communication. And by a problem of communication I mean that we do not understand each other. It is absurd to believe that we don't understand each other because one is good and the other is bad or vice versa; both parties want the best for all. They don't understand each other because their positions are still dialectical.

Dialectical thought has made the Industrial Revolution possible; there is nothing wrong with it. But now it is time to change it because the competition and the opposition which was necessary during that period—which was absolutely necessary then—is now, in the moment we are living, totally unnecessary. We can compete no more. The territory of our planet is too well known. All the experts in all the areas are saying exactly the same thing, that this planet is limited, and we must start thinking in terms of good administration of its limited resources. If radiation will not kill us, the bad allocation of resources will!

So I would say that this lack of communication is really a lack of understanding. I am not exaggerating the word—I am just saying *lack of understanding*. There is no lack of goodwill—both sides have goodwill. Nobody wants to die.

Q: We have organizations like the World Wildlife Fund and ecological organizations that tell everyone that various things are being threatened by extinction. We know, for example, that the Amazon basin, which provides half the world's oxygen produced by land plants, is being destroyed by chopping down all the trees. So the world, with all its technological improvements in communication, knows about these things. The crazy thing is that, even though the individual knows about the problem, it still continues. We only have four thousand tigers left, but people are still killing them. So why doesn't the individual person do something, or why doesn't society take a look at those problems?

OSCAR: Well again, you know, it is because we don't agree about what we want of this planet. We don't agree about that exploitation.... Well, we do agree, in that everybody now agrees that exploitation for the sake of exploitation should stop. But at the same time no one wants to give it up, as you pointed out very well.

I want to stress again that only a new way of reasoning can provide us with that tool of intercommunication and understanding. And this new way of reasoning is really a logic, a new logic which will deal with the 'unity' of the process rather than with the process in itself.

Dialectical thought, as we know very well, explains change. But change by itself is not an endless line of change. Change does exist, but it exists in cycles that are preestablished. So you have at the same time something permanent, the cycle, and something which changes, and they are not contradictory. That would be what I call 'trialectics', or the 'logic of the unity'.

Q: You seem to be saying that there's a philosophical way of thinking that will help us get through the present world crisis. Is that what you're saying?

OSCAR: Exactly. Because of the growth of science, mostly in the last century, and at the beginning of ours, there was a total resentment with the word 'metaphysics'. You know, metaphysics became something of a dirty word. It came to be like this because metaphysics failed to make us understand the world as it really is. It became a type of, let's say, dilettante thought, you know, a game one played with his own mind;

and everybody who considered himself a scientist would tend to say, "I am opposed to metaphysics." So, you know, all that has discredited the terms of philosophy.

And on the other side you can see what, precisely, metaphysics did. Marxism comes directly from metaphysics. It *is* metaphysics. It is continually dealing with the problems of metaphysics, with the root problems of metaphysics. Well, that is what Marxism is. Marxism really insists that it presents a materialistic point of view, contradicting its position with an idealistic position.

But what we are saying here is that philosophy is not a dilettante's game. On the contrary, it is what establishes the principles of how we think and it establishes the climate in which science can progress. We cannot really think about modern mathematics and physics without thinking deeply about the thought of Bertrand Russell. It is with him, you know, that the approach to logic came in terms of mathematics. In his *Principia* he was trying to make a bridge with mathematical logic and what already had been discovered in physics, which our logic could not, let's say, grasp. What I want to say is that Bertrand Russell, you know, began a large movement in philosophy which now includes all the dialecticians.

But anyhow, the problem is that a new philosophy, a new point of view, must appear, and must appear now.

Q: Let's pause here for a moment. Would you mind explaining to me what dialectics and trialectics are? I mean, does the world move basically as the result of cause and effect?

OSCAR: Thank you.

Well, dialectical thought explains change. How? With three principles that we all know. Let's review very quickly.

'Quantity becomes quality'; a quantity of heat added to water causes a qualitative change. The water becomes vapor. Then there is the 'law of opposites'; there is night and day, there's heat and cold, there's love and hate, etc. And there is the principle of the 'negation of the negation' which means that every process, for continuing as a process, must deny itself like the seed must cease to be a seed as it becomes a tree, etc.

Now, the proposition of trialectics is to establish not only the fact of change, that the change exists, but that change is not random, is not, let's say, a coincidence. Change is pre-established, as for example, the seasonal changes of the year are pre-established; there is summer, there is winter, etc. There are the seasons. The changes of the moon as it moves around the earth are pre-established. Every change is then pre-established. There is a moment for us to be infants, and then children, and then becoming adolescents is pre-established. We do not become adolescent when we are thirty years old. The moment is pre-established, the moment when it happens organically. It also happens organically that we come into maturity, which occurs when we are not going to grow any more, and that's that. It is a pre-established point, and the change is there.

So we must understand, then, that we see two conditions in our world, I mean, in our external world: the condition that there is change, and the condition that there is a pre-established point where change will occur.

Q: Is it the fact that there are pre-established points, or the recognition of pre-established points, that makes the jump from dialectics to trialectics?

OSCAR: It is precisely that. Because, for example, it has already been very well established in quantum theory that everything changes in jumps. Nature is not a gradual accumulation of accidents. On the contrary, it is something that produces itself in jumps, as for example, the shells of the electrons as viewed from the theory of Niels Bohr; we know very well that they expand and contract in jumps. There are no 'in-betweens'. Now, according to dialectical predictions, there should be 'in-betweens', there should be a crescendo style of change which does not exist in reality. Instead, change occurs from one point to the other. We know very well, from quantum theory, that photons can be absorbed by the nucleus only if they are of the proper size. So it is pre-established again.

Q: Just to clarify things, can you give me an example of this philosophy working in society? I assume that you are saying dialectics is the way society thinks now, and that we have to make a jump to trialectics.

OSCAR: It would be working when we have the recognition that our world is not our invention, that we are a humanity which is growing in a pre-established sequence to a pre-established result. The crisis we are living in is not because we are bad. It is because it is part of the historical process.

Philosophy will begin working in society when we begin understanding that the challenge we face is precisely what will make us jump to another level of understanding, another level of humanity. This is something that we must have confidence in, or really this is disaster already.

But there is more. You know, when I speak about change, when I speak about jumps, I have been using the word 'challenge', the same word that Arnold Toynbee used for describing how cultures are produced. Cultures are produced because there is a challenge to accomplish. And I would say there couldn't be a clearer definition of what I call trialectics, in the sense of history changing.

Q: Surely you are not saying the kind of conflict that exists between NATO and the Communist bloc is pre-established and is there as a challenge in order for society to make a jump.

OSCAR: Inevitably we must think in that way, you know, strange as it could seem.

But you know, NATO and all that—and, well—the opposite side, the Warsaw Pact—all that is a happening of history. Nobody invented these things for playing games with them. It just happens that they happen. They happen because they are on opposite sides. They want to defend their own interests in whatever way they interpret the word, and so on.

Q: Are we just going to have more and more superpowers? For example, is Europe with the EEC just going to be another superpower?

OSCAR: Well, it is absolutely necessary for that to happen because it would create equilibrium, equilibrium in the sense that wherever it would move would define the side. Now, this is not a strange thought; it is already that way. European industry would then be an integrated industry, completely organized as one solid sequence. It becomes immediately the most gigantic pole with the advantage that Europe has *real* relations with the Third World. So it would therefore attract the money of the Third World, and the possibilities of the Third World, and they would be very well served in return. No doubt about it.

Q: I am not sure what you are saying. Are you saying that there is more unity among the labor force than there is among the governments?

OSCAR: No. But I am saying this: the labor force of Europe has a common history. From the very beginning, the labor force has been serving its own nationalisms. But that game is over.

There is also in the labor force an understanding that unity is absolutely important if European nations are to survive as industrial powers, or as industrial nations if you want, because the resulting superpower would no doubt be the consortium of them all.

Q: I can't see how a philosophy can possibly change the world. When I look at man's history, ever since he has been Homo sapiens, he has always had his territory and there have always been territorial conflicts. It seems to me that all that is happening with NATO and the Communist bloc is that the territorial game is simply bigger now. Are you saying that man can make the jump out of that whole history of conflicts to another kind of society?

OSCAR: Indeed, it looks utopian and it looks completely

out of reality and perhaps even naive; but it has to happen because it is the only solution we have. It is not a matter now of merely desire or goodwill. It is a matter of survival. Again, the game is over in the sense of competition, in the sense of trying to have the bigger part of the cake and so on.

Q: Excuse me for a moment for being a little cynical. But society is surely fairly dogmatic and conservative in its way of thinking. I mean, how do you envisage seeing your new theory being accepted in time to avoid the present crisis?

OSCAR: For an example anyhow, you know, the most sensitive part of our society is indeed the young people, the youth, because whatever trouble comes, they are going to be the ones finally who are involved. Excuse me for being cynical on my part, but that is how it is. So, you know, they are most concerned with these types of matters.

There is also a great wave of understanding between the younger generations in both blocs, precisely because they know they are going to be confronting one another. There have been already too many tragedies, and unfortunately the war in Vietnam has been a tremendous lesson, in the sense that we cannot go to war just because we want to go to war. We cannot do just what we want because we have decided that's the way to do it. The problem is always this: the younger generations are the ones who pay most dearly; they have to support the effort. And if I were to put myself in their shoes I would be screaming too, if you want.

Q: What is the relationship between youth or the energy of youth and the maturity of an older person?

OSCAR: Well, each age has its own beauty and its own excellence. There is no beautiful age and no ugly age. That's absurd. But, you know, what happens is that the older generations always try to lead the younger generations in how they would want them to be. So in a certain way this is a frustration; they are trying to impose their ways on the younger ones. But the younger ones have their own purpose, their own history, their own momentum, and their own way of thinking. This could be clarified and that would make an understanding between the generations, determining the role of each. Each age in our life has its own purpose. And it is equally the same in a society. Each generation has to make its own purpose.

Q: Has society, like a human being, grown from the beginning to an adolescence and to a maturity?

OSCAR: Exactly.

Well, I would really not like to make, you know, a gross analogy. I'm really trying to extend all the possibilities of analogical thought to the extreme, but it happens that both are the same type of process. Indeed, we must think of humanity as only one body. At the end that's how it has to happen or we will not survive. These are very simple terms and we know them very well. I mean everybody knows what I am speaking about. In this sense it is an obvious reality; it is not an idealistic point of view. So, we must think of humanity as being really one body and one spirit. But now here again this may look, I don't know, totally idealistic and theoretical, but it's not. Again, you know, it's simply part of our process. We can then say that in the moment of maturity, when we become mature, the adventures of external discovery are over. And we will become completely responsible, recognizing our own limitations.

Q: But when I look at society at the moment, I see high unemployment, conflicts with the law, labor relations problems, a lack of understanding between the old and the young. I mean, isn't it hard to think of humanity rather than ourselves as coming first?

OSCAR: Well, strange as it could seem at first glance, both positions are equally necessary. You know, it is a dichotomous position and whenever there is a dichotomy, it's not that there is contradiction between the terms; what must happen instead is equilibrium between them. It is exactly, you know, as in a fractional balance scale, where both sides must be equally well provided for, with the same weight.

Q: As well as philosophy, what are the other aspects to what you're trying to do?

OSCAR: Well, to answer briefly, if we have a philosophical point of view of clarity, all our sciences will be the first beneficiaries. It's always been this way, of course. That's the purpose, necessarily, of philosophy.

Q: What would be the result on an individual of adopting your logic?

OSCAR: Well, here I don't really want to sound boastful, claiming things for myself or for this theory. But it happens that when we have a clear point of view, we ourselves, and all our actions, improve at the same time. So, I guess that is what I think about it—okay?

Q: We've been talking in general terms on a world scale about problems. Let's bring it down to an individual level. If I think of us as ordinary people, we're always full of confusions—you know, during the day we don't know how to make a decision between this thing and that thing. We worry about what our bosses are thinking about us and we forget things and we don't seem to get organized and we worry and we fret and we have regrets and worry about the past. I mean, surely, as individuals we need somehow to get ourselves together before we can start solving society's problems. So, does the individual need to get himself together before we can solve society's problems?

OSCAR: Well, indeed you know this: every time a human being becomes better, society becomes better; that is certain. That's something that we all know well and we all recognize perfectly well. So what happens is this: society becomes the projection of human beings and not the reverse.

Of course, every human being will be, let's say, molded by society, because usually a human being starts assimilating his culture, but he does not develop it. He doesn't develop the language that he speaks. He does not develop the taste which is already there. He does not develop the history that's already there. In one word, he does not develop the culture that he lives in. But in the other side, that culture will have, by the way, another vitality or another life if there are individuals capable of recognizing themselves, because they will help the culture develop.

So, finally in a few words, what I am trying to say here is that the individual, if he really improves himself, will immediately improve his own society. But these are things that will start happening only on the individual level. If there is, however, a social, let's say, acceptance of that individual process, so much the better. Perhaps it is the only way this can happen, because I don't see how the individual is going to do it if there is a total social opposition to what he is doing.

Q: Are you proposing some kind of theory or method that will help individuals sort themselves out, as it were?

OSCAR: Every epoch or every culture has always had its own ways of self-realization and its own ways of becoming better, or its own ways of really achieving the best from life. Our times, of course, need a similar method, and it is born out of the new parameters that our history and our society present to us. And this method must understand and accommodate the complexity of the society we are living in. There are no simple answers to this question. On the contrary, it must be an entire system, totally coordinated, specifically categorized, and scientifically proved as being efficient, as being capable of fulfilling the job that it is supposed to.

Q: You're putting forward an idea of a unified system. But if I look, say, at the birth of science with, say, philosophy, philosophy has grown into several disciplines of psychology, sociology, linguistics; and the universities are full of many, many departments all trying to understand society and human beings. How can you now bring that all together into one system? It seems too big and too complex.

OSCAR: Well, it is indeed that big and that complex, no doubt about it. You know, it is the common effort of every philosopher and every academic (whatever his field may be) to understand the unity between what he is doing and to integrate it with the entire intellectual cosmos, so to speak, where he has got to live and to be. You know, ever since the time of Thales of Miletus, and Parmenides, Anaximenes, and Anaximander, all of them are questioning philosophy precisely as a means of interpreting nature, because finally that's what philosophy is.

Philosophy begins when we question nature and we question the universe as something separate from ourselves. Before that moment we are just in a religious position or in a magical position of understanding. We are related with the universe. We do not question it. But what comes immediately with philosophy is that it questions not only the reality that is 'living' but it also questions what is 'being', the fundamental being. What is 'to be'? What is permanent? What is random? What is the unity of the process we are living?

Q: Are you saying that nature has evolved to a position where we now have on the planet a form of life that can actually witness the universe, that can actually see itself? I mean, why, how would the universe create that kind of energy that would want to be able to see itself? I mean, it's almost as if human beings can now, for the first time, reason and contemplate the existence of the universe and their own existence.

OSCAR: Again, we have to recognize that all nature and all of what we know as evolution are again the product of separate jumps to very concrete points. For example, the jumps between the animal genera from one form to another in the scale of evolution: no doubt there is a very well established scale already. It's very easy to see the jumps, as for example, between birds and mammals, etc. There is a jump to something totally different but still there is a sequence.

But, you know, it's like the old 'spirit of nature' is leading necessarily to that one species which is the human being and in that sense, indeed, human beings are the product of all that is below them in the scale. So, again we must imagine the world and we must imagine humanity as being a product of a a process, and this product at this time has to have its own product, so to speak. That is, humanity is now evolving to become a single humanity rather than several special interests with all the divisions that we know in the world.

Q: How are we going to achieve, as it were, an understanding between all human beings? Is that a possibility?

OSCAR: Well, our need of survival is what is putting us in the need for that comprehension, so it is something that just has to happen—historically. And we all are in the effort of trying for that.

Q: Let's go a bit more specifically with your theory. How does your theory relate to the present world situation?

OSCAR: Well, what happens is that this theory tries to start with establishing a logic that functions with science, and at the same time interprets science, and that evolves to the concept of the unity of the human process, the unity of a human life.

At this point what we have are merely 'ideas' of what we are; we have only ideas and beliefs about what we want.

But the universe is already pre-established in the sense that everything has its own limitations. We have now touched our own limitations. And that makes us desire external conquest less violently. Now we also have the desire of making the conquest of our internal universe. This is of course something that everybody knows and speaks about.

Q: It looks like we have a double-barreled advantage from doing something that's going to get ourselves together. Not only will we be better as people, as it were, and enjoy life, but also we can help the whole of humanity at the same time. Is that what you're saying?

OSCAR: Precisely and exactly. That's that. Thank you.

Q: In the seventeenth century, Francis Bacon restated the notion that knowledge of God could come by direct revelation and by reason. Is your theory the same in this respect?

OSCAR: No doubt about it. I would say not only Bacon but all the major philosophers agreed on that point. It is an effort of trying to understand our soul and mysticism in terms of reason. That's what philosophy is all about. And there is also, you know, the contradiction between mysticism and reason. It looks as if one denies the other. Francis Bacon did envision that reason and mysticism in reality are two polarities of the same game. I agree with that, but mine is a different point of explanation. He had one way of logic, which corresponds to dialectical logic, and I am proposing a new one.

Q: But it looks to me as though man's reason is getting him more into trouble than it is helping him.

OSCAR: Oh, no. That happens because the existing logic of our time is obsolete. So we must accept that we need a new logic. We need new terms for interrelating with one another and understanding one another. We cannot continue in a situation where we believe that we produce historical events. It's not that simple.

In reality what happens is that we are a product of nature rather than the invention of our own criteria. If that were the case we would be living in paradise and everybody would have his own paradise, and it's not like that. What happens is that we have to live under the propositions and under the terms of reality—I mean of an objective reality which is what made us—and not in reverse.

Q: Would you describe seeing objective reality as like conscience? You know, it's like we have a saying, "Always let your conscience be your guide." Is that what's going to give an objective reality?

OSCAR: No. Because, well, first, conscience is not something we have gratuitously. It is something that we have to clarify; it is something that we have to make so clear that it can reabsorb reality objectively rather than through the propositions of our mind. Normally what happens is that we assemble a subjective world rather than absorb the objective world which is more understandable in terms of society.

Q: Let's move to psychology for a moment. In the same way that you say society has limits, you have said that the human mind has limits too. How did you discover the patterns that exist in your maps of the human psyche, for example, the series of nine that seem to prevail?

OSCAR: Well, this is just the simple observation of the external reality. Everything is the product of light—it certainly is—and light seems to behave in a cycle of nine. Even though we can see the spectrum in a linear way, it is not linear. The spectrum is circular, that is, it behaves in cycles rather than in linear fashion.

Anyhow, every process we see in nature can be divided into a sequence of nine stages. It would be a wonder if the human psyche and the human organism would be different. The cycle of nine is just following universal reality, and it fits.

Q: You describe the new society which we need in order that humanity may survive as a metasociety. What is a metasociety?

OSCAR: Well, society as we have known it until today is a collection of individuals who have a common sense of organization in terms of their survival and in terms of prosperity. Let's say that present day societies serve the individual.

What we need is a new society which really understands that we must serve society in order to serve ourselves. That is, if we proceed with individualistic or egoistic propositions, of course we are in trouble, since blind competition will lead us to imbalance.

Q: So what will the metasociety be like? I mean, would we have one kind of culture, for example?

OSCAR: Well, it will be a society which is composed of all the various parts which make up humanity, respecting everyone, you know, for their own special characteristics, their own point of view, and even, I would say, reconstructing their traditions and making them even more meaningful than they are today. But at the same time, they should be in mutual accord with what humanity wants, so that we don't compete destructively, but, on the contrary, we cooperate.

This is not a new point of view either, but it is the dream of every economist and the dream of every sociologist, as well as being the dream of every individual on the planet.

Q: But we don't even have unity amongst religions. I mean, if religions are about some kind of love for humanity, then things have gone crazy, because, for example, in Northern Ireland, two Christian groups, the Catholics and the Protestants, have been fighting for several years. And, for example, the Christians say the only way to recognize or realize God is through Christ. So how are we going to get unity on the planet if even the religions don't have unity within themselves?

OSCAR: Well, unity is possible if we really understand what our psyche is composed of and we know what our society is composed of.

What I mean is this: The contradictions we have are the result of our incomplete understanding of ourselves. Well, now, this may have the appearance of a tremendous claim. But this theory proposes to clarify the human psyche in such a way that we can all come into accord in defining what the psyche is, because up to this point in history we don't even know what psychosis is. We don't know. We don't have a workable definition of psychosis or what provokes it. Most of the time we are just dealing with *words* rather than with reality, because we ignore the defects of our definitions. That is the reality of the situation, whether we want to acknowledge it or not. That's how it is.

Q: Well, what's gone wrong then? I mean, it would almost seem that human beings take better care of their cars than they do of themselves. How does that come about?

OSCAR: Well, that is obviously changing, since there has come lately a sudden rush of understanding that diet is very important. I have been saying strongly that you are exactly what you eat. It has now become a very popular phrase. But it's not that simple either, you know. We must realize that diet is a science. Many authorities now are explaining this with more and more data. And we also now see a rush for athletics and for really taking care of the body because we understand that a human being is really an organism and must be treated as an organism, and not as a machine, because it is certainly not that.

Q: Let's go back a little. You have said, in the past, that there have been many previous rediscoveries of the unity. And yet we are in an even bigger crisis than before. How is humanity ever going to get enlightened?

OSCAR: Well, the discovery of the unity is the discovery of God. But each time, we discover God in our own dimensions and for our own purposes. There's nothing wrong with that. But our time needs to rediscover unity. This seems comical to speak of—you know, once you discover the unity, that's that. You know, it may look absurd, but nevertheless, each historical period has—and I insist on this point—to rediscover God. And in our time of history we have to rediscover God in terms of science. There we would have a real science for sure. We would then understand the Eternal.

I am not the first in saying this, you know. There are too many essays being published now which predict the inevitable proximity of a new mathematics which can incorporate simple, plain mysticism. Now, this is not news. So you see, we have to rediscover the unity again. We are in the process, no doubt about it. We didn't finish that process, though. Because if we would be finished, we would all agree in the points and the parameters and variables that we are considering.

Q: Surely you're not saying there's a scientific method toward getting enlightened?

OSCAR: Sure, I am saying that.

Q: Obviously what you propose is a scientific method. Do you intend to put your method to the scientific and academic communities for criticism?

OSCAR: Well, naturally. That's the function of science, you know.

Q: Do you think that when the scientific community receives your theory that they will in fact in some way maybe refine it or sharpen it through an interchange, a dialogue between your theory and the academicians?

OSCAR: Well, of course, you know, it's got to be like that; that's what every theory desires. But, you know, if it is to have any value, that will be seen. It will be criticized for sure; this has to happen in every process of the academy. That's where things really get refined, no doubt.

Q: In order for society to change, does it require everyone to adopt your new theory?

OSCAR: No, absolutely not. That's not necessary at all. But I *would* say that if I am going to speak specifically of laws, I mean of laws that work in nature and work in the psyche too, well that's that. I am not saying that everybody is going to be converted. But it is like any other description—for example, that the atom is in some form—and once we discover it is like that, then that's that.

But with this knowledge we will be able to refer to ourselves better.

Q: As well as developing your theory, you have also become a spiritual teacher. What made you decide to pass on your experience in this way?

OSCAR: Well, I elaborated this theory, how to 'read' the human psyche and understand its complex mechanism which can be seen across very specific parameters which give us a clear conceptualization of a human being. Once this was in my hands, there came a natural inclination on my part to try and pass this knowledge to others, nothing more natural, really. So with enormous limitations on my part, at the beginning, I started teaching around 1956. But at that point my teaching consisted rather more of traditional paths and traditional methods than my own methods which were completed in 1960. Until then it was still a process of elaboration, so I would discuss rather than teach, and it was more a kind of seminar than a lecture process.

In 1960, I began teaching what we know as trialectics, because it was completed then and the entire system was complete. But it was not until 1967 that I decided it was necessary to found a school to pass this instruction to a larger number of people who, once they had this type of instruction, in due time would be able to or would be capable of transmitting it to others. But this type of thing can only be done in a school, understanding the term 'school' in the mystical sense, which is a body of people who coordinate themselves and become a nucleus, or an organism which lives, functions, and has all the particulars of an individual. Because a school becomes a 'social individual'.

So, if you see, Alfie, it has been a process which started first in my trying to pass my experiences to others. In a second stage, the situation became that of building a school instead of just having a group.

Before, I worked with groups; it was not a school, it was not an organism. So when the group of fifty Americans came to Arica, for the first time I really worked in order to found a school with, of course, the parameters and the techniques needed until you have produced this organism, this individual, this social individual.

Q: What, fundamentally, is the purpose of your teaching?

OSCAR: Well, I declare very clearly that Arica is a mystical school, so in that way the purpose of the entire teaching is finally to unite ourselves with the Eternal Creator, which is, by the way, the only goal of any true mysticism.

Q: Did you ever consider working within an academic framework, say, out of a university?

OSCAR: Indeed, this is very important, because if this teaching is true and scientific, as I say it is, it should be natural to work in that academic framework.

So this, let's say, is a consequence of the type of instruction that we pass in Arica. We are not working on the basis of faith, but rather on the basis of our intellect, however contradictory it appears at this point. As we have said before in the interview, the intellect has always been considered by mystics as something which disturbs our unity with the Eternal rather than helps that unity. So it is strange at this point to say that we can do it, that we can really achieve our total realization, on the basis of our intellect. But of course that must be true if we have discovered all the parameters and all the possibilities of our intellect. This, again, is very hard to accept at first sight, because we like to consider our intellect to be infinite. We like to believe that our possibilities in the rational world are limitless. Well, in fact it is not like that. And that is what Arica seeks to explain or, let's say, that is the most fundamental point. Let's say that this is the real news in Arica, the real news of Arica.

Q: You have said that you have accumulated a vast amount of knowledge from those various traditions that have as their common goal placing man in tune with his universe. How did you formalize your teaching from this experience?

OSCAR: I said somewhere else that the mystical experience happens to us when and only when our cortex, our cerebral cortex, becomes unified or becomes harmonized in such a way that it immediately starts working on a different level—in a totally different level. More clearly, it is like this: We can have a mystical experience once there comes to us this complete pacification of our mind, or this complete unification or this total tranquillity of mind. In such a way our mind really starts going to the lowest vibrations in the EEG scale. More clearly, we know very well that there exist four types of waves that we can read in the electroencephalogram, the alpha wave, the beta wave—then the theta and the delta waves.

So, as we can see, the lower frequency indicates the higher state. Everybody agrees that the state of meditation is produced by the alpha wave. But if we descend to the theta wave we can produce even higher states. And the delta wave is known as being the wave of a state of coma, that is really when we are already deprived of sensorial input and we are living in an interior condition, so to speak. But what happens is that the highest states of mysticism or the highest experiences in mysticism occur precisely when we touch this wave or when we can produce it. That is when all the activities of our cerebral cortex have been pacified in a way that then it is one unity and one solid experience of our entire being.

Now, again, these types of experiences are completely different from the normal ones that we have. So, at first they are immensely striking for us, and they convince us that we live in a universe that is ordered and is perfect. And, moreover, we know that we can return to that perfection; we can return to our Creator.

So I would say, once more, that in every mystical tradition the teaching is precisely to train people to that point where they can reproduce in themselves this state of totality of the cerebral cortex. So that's why in, for example, all the teachings of Zen, what they want is to pacify the mind, and for that the whole exercise is just sitting down and trying not to think.

Now here again it seems contradictory that we claim in Arica that we can reproduce intellectually this state of the totality of the cerebral cortex. But in fact we want to achieve that state of totality not by denying the intellect but by using the intellect as an instrument to achieve that situation or that condition in the cortex. That means, again, that we must know all the parameters of our mind, how it works, and how to use it to our benefit rather than in our disturbance.

Q: Is what you are presenting something new or a cocktail derived from other methods?

OSCAR: Well, Alfie, in the beginning, during the ten-month training in Arica, the first seven months of the teaching comprised about sixty percent traditional methods and about forty percent new Arica techniques. And I went like that because first I wanted to review what the traditions could offer us and because, you know, those students were very serious and very knowledgeable about these traditions; they had done various types of methods and traditions, and were really very well informed. But just because that information was there I saw that it was necessary for us first, if we were going to become a school and a mystical individual with unity of thought in a school, that we have a solid foundation for continuing which would give us the necessary clarity for what we were doing.

Well, anyhow, because of that Arica was seen, at the beginning, as a cocktail of things. That, of course, was not my intention at all. Another thing is this: that every tradition must be worked separately because each is a complete unity.

You cannot make a cocktail of traditions. That is totally false. I was not doing that at all. At any time I would teach one distinct path, just that path without including any elements of a different path. Or more clearly, suppose: If we were doing some Sufi exercise we would be working that Sufi exercise exclusively, not mixing Sufism with yoga, or yoga with Zen, etc. We worked them as separate units and never really mixed them. We were studying these traditions, just as you can study geography, mathematics, or history, and yet you don't confuse them; each is a different science with a different method.

So in the beginning there was the inclination to believe we were that type of cocktail, and somehow this triggered other groups to start with what we can call cocktails of mysticism, which of course become spurious. I would say I distrust those types of mixtures. Let's say, from my point of view, I distrust them because I know by experience that each of the traditions, as I say, is a complete method, is a total unit that must be worked within those parameters which have been accepted by that tradition.

Now, because Arica belongs to our culture, belongs to our time, it is the last school, the last serious school.

I want to put an accent here. It is the last serious school that has appeared in our civilization. This is totally necessary to happen. Arica is not the product just of my mind; it is the product of our needs, it is the product of our times; it belongs to our time; it answers the questions of our time; and more than anything, it opens a new way to approach mysticism, a way that is much easier because it is logical, intellectual, and *reasonable*.

The traditional paths go by irrational terms. And they are

irrational precisely because you have to jump reason and get inside of total faith, as Søren Kierkegaard pointed out so well. Here of course, I am speaking of the *Knight of Faith*, the one who will jump over the abyss that exists between faith and reason. He will accept faith in a totally blind situation, with completeness and totality, as in the case that he pointed to about the faith of Abraham who was totally secure of his orders—or the message that he had from the Divine.

In this sense, you know, the proposition of Arica is, as I said in another part of the interview, to open a new path. And because it is the most human one, it is the most available, and it is the easiest, since we don't have to start solidly upon faith. Thank you.

Q: What is a mystical school and what do mystical schools have in common?

OSCAR: Well, as I said, a mystical school is a social unity, a social body, a social individual. And I say 'individual' because we can really individualize that group or that number of people, not as an aggregate of simple numbers, but because they have a common basis for existence as a social 'individual'. Now, what all mystical schools have in common is that they have the same purpose. They are built on the basis that we can understand what is divine and we can approach and realize the mystical union.

Q: Is the Arica School the same in this respect?

OSCAR: Absolutely.

Q: What is the advantage of working within a school framework?

OSCAR: The immense advantage is that in the first work of a mystical school the tradition, or the body of teaching, is respected and cared for. That is one part.

The other and no less important aspect is that when we work in social connection and we are interacting as human beings, our internal self becomes energized by the presence or the sum of consciousness, and in this sense this social body becomes a complete and total union.

We say in Arica that humanity is one body and humanity is one spirit, and we mean it. But it is even stronger in the Arica School. Arica is a real unity. We are one in Arica; we are one body and one spirit that has been clarifying itself. These types of schools have been built objectively, in the sense that they really respect the internal laws of how these organisms can be created and be conducted. The advantage is that when you work in such a framework, your will to succeed is almost guaranteed because you see the example of others achieving certain levels and states that you too can achieve immediately.

Q: Is the Arica School in the line of any particular tradition?

OSCAR: Well, precisely because, as I say, the Arica School came from a totally new point of view, it doesn't respond, or is not rooted in any other tradition. In this sense the Arica School is totally new; it is totally original and, of course, it is totally independent.

Q: You have stated that one of the purposes of Arica is 'ego reduction'. What does this mean?

OSCAR: Well, via a natural process we develop in ourselves what we have seen in this theory as three different egos. What happens is that these egos are fixated or, let's say, they have created barriers around us. And these barriers become so extreme that in the end we are not living objectively in the world, but our own barriers stand between us and reality. So, inasmuch as we reduce the framework of barriers that these three egos place around us, we can realize what is objective and we can live in reality with a solid point of view. Thank you.

Q: One accepted method of achieving this is through devotion to a guru. Is your relationship with the School in any way like this?

OSCAR: No. Absolutely not. I have been very clear from the beginning of all this in saying that I am not a guru. And my intention here is not, of course, in any way to be disrespectful with guruship. Not at all. I accept its existence and the need in the world is very obvious, but in our world, and here specifically I am speaking of the super-industrialized countries, we need a totally new method that can make our technologies work for us instead of destroy us. Here I am referring to this nightmare of machines controlling men. Here I would remember for example Hal in the Kubrick film. And of course, you know, there comes to mind immediately Orson Welles and H.G. Wells and so many others.

But I want to say here that what we do have is a common nightmare. Science and machines are sooner or later going to overwhelm us. We really should give that nightmare a second thought. Because, if we see, science and the development of atomic explosions are our worst enemy at this point. And we are in danger of disappearing as a race and of liquidating ourselves and committing suicide.

So, if we see that the methods, the traditional methods, do not defend us against this reality, only if we make our science and our intellect part of our evolution, will it then make sense and be positive for us.

Q: How is Arica going to cope with the resistance people have to organized groups that lack conventional and academic credentials?

OSCAR: Well, every new idea, until it becomes accepted by society, has to have a period of process and testing, so to speak. In that sense, Arica has been tested during the ten years since the School was founded.

It's been almost fifteen years since I started with instruction in the Arica method. Well, in reality your question, Alfie, is a matter of credentials, and those credentials are provided only by reality and by the results that the method produces, and by how reasonable it is and how logical it is. For us it is precisely on the basis of logic that we structure this path. Because, once more, it is absolutely more difficult to accept paths that are built upon irrational types of thought. I am not saying that such paths do not exist and are not real. I am saying that they start in irrational terms. For example, magic is irrational, and mysticism, until now, has been based, as I said before, on irrational terms.

Here 'irrational' doesn't mean bad or wrong. It just means that it goes beyond reason for achieving direct experience, that that is what we are talking about in mysticism, meaning that, well, the mind has got to be overpowered, or if you like, it has to be jumped over or has to be circumvented. Thank you.

Q: Even though there are no rules and regulations, Aricans have a certain lifestyle. What are the key principles that members of the School employ in their day-to-day lives?

OSCAR: Okay. Well, as you say, Alfie, there is a style in the Arica School, a style that is the outcome of certain types of exercises that we do regularly, because we have what we call our daily routine, that, as you said very well, is not an order or a must for being in the School but is indeed a tremendous help. Because, as we know very well, if things are performed in order and in sequence it is inevitable that we will have a better result. In this sense, perhaps the most important thing here is that because they are living under different parameters, Aricans have a different attitude to life, to their society, and to the surrounding universe.

Q: What has been the influence of the Arica School in society since it was founded in 1971?

OSCAR: Without any intention of being grandiose about Arica, I can say in a very direct way that we have really influenced this society deeply, more deeply perhaps than outsiders would accept and even what Aricans accept about their influence on society.

But there is no doubt that Arica has started a whole new way in the human potential movement, because until the moment Arica came into existence, most of the paths were Oriental and very few were Western, and those that were Western were immensely influenced by the Oriental ideas. So, I can say distinctly that Arica is one of the very few traditions or methods to be born in the Western culture. In that sense Arica has also triggered the appearance of other groups that seem to have the direct influence of Arica in the sense that Western culture can produce indeed its own methods.

Q: Where do you see the School going from here?

OSCAR: It has to realize for what it has been created and for what it has been organized, which is to give or to take the Arica methods and the Arica system to the widest possible spectrum of society that it can.

But it is more than that, because what we say is that Arica is a mission. It's a mission in the sense of the survival of humanity, so we are really speaking in very, very, very deep terms. And again, Alfie, every time that we speak of humanity, immediately it sounds grandiose. It sounds overwhelming. It sounds pretentious, if you like. But we mean seriously what we say and I am certain that if we just count on the benevolent attention of our society, Arica is going to accomplish what it has been founded for, for what it has been, you know, structured until now. Thank you very much.

INDEX

OSCAR ICHAZO was born in Roboré, Bolivia, in 1931, was educated in La Paz and Lima, and earned his living for many years as a writer and journalist. At the age of nineteen, he was appointed director of Bolivia's Library of Congress. At twenty-three, he studied with a group of mystics in Buenos Aires who then made it possible for him to continue his work with master teachers in the Middle and Far East. He began teaching in Latin America in 1960, and in 1971 he founded the Arica Institute in New York. He is currently at work on the definitive book of the Arica theory and method.